ASTROMUSIK

EZRA SANDZER-BELL

2014 SYNC BOOK PRESS

ASTROMUSIK

EZRA SANDZER-BELL

SYNC BOOK PRESS

SYNCBOOKPRESS.COM

Cover artwork and illustrations on pages
86, 94, 141, 144, 147, 148, 150, 151, 157, 181
by Danlyn Brennan

Interior layout by Ezra Sandzer-Bell

Cover design work by Alan Abbadessa-Green

Published 2014 Sync Book Press : New York — San Francisco
ISBN-13: 978-0692022665
ISBN-10: 069202266x

Acknowledgments

This book is the product of seven years of research and the support of countless friends and allies. A living example of the Harmony of the Spheres, it demonstrates how numerous converging influences can come together in life and make something happen that otherwise would have been impossible.

My deepest gratitude goes out to my grandmother, Jacqueline Bell, for her unrivaled generosity of spirit. To my mother and father for never putting me down or telling me I was crazy to be studying these topics. Also to my dear friend and mentor Paul Levy, who was there with me every step of the way. To Danlyn Brennan, who lovingly supported the creative process and contributed numerous original illustrations to this book. And finally, to my editorial crew, Karen Mark and Keith for all of their contributions and insights.

An extra special thanks goes out to Casey Burge, Steve Willner, Lance Lightsmith, and Jason Horsley for their comradery and support during the early, transitional years of this research. For giving me a platform to share my voice while it was still developing, a warm thanks to Henrik Palmgrien of Red Ice Creations, Greg Kaminsky of Occult of Personality, and Alan Green of the Sync Book Press.

A big thanks to all of my relations in Portland, including the Sound Grounds crew and Harmony Studios, the Awakening in the Dream community, OneDoorLand, Mitch and the Living Maya, Daniel Flessas @ KBOO, and the Minden allstars. Thank you Cassandra for tipping me off to black cohosh, Maria Allred for assisting with the photographs, Whelky for contributing the Scott Rogo connection, and Roberta Ma for the Kabbalistic tip. Lots of love to my Midwest family: Asher, Kyle, Sarah, and Amelia Delia Maj, along with the original gentlemen, Brandon Knocke, Robbie Beffort, and Andrew Heuback.

Props to the authors at Original Falcon Press: Antero Alli, Robert Anton Wilson, Israel Regardie, Chris Hyatt, and Timothy Leary. Also a special thanks to Joscelyn Godwin, who gave me the historical backbone to have faith in my research, and to Paul Foster Case for blowing the whistle on the Golden Dawn's hidden musical elements.

Harmonic Order of the Golden Song

- Table of Contents -

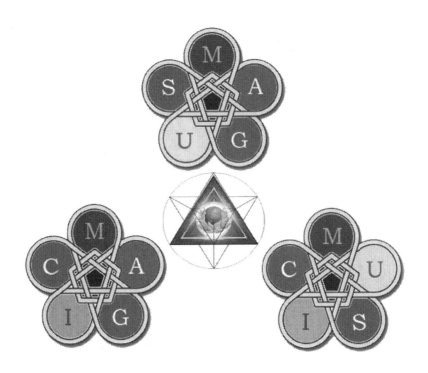

M.M.M.

3 9

Music, Myth, and Magick

The strangest thing about music, without a doubt, is the immediate and powerful effect that it has upon human consciousness. Anyone can listen to it and feel a deep response in their body. The very act of listening affects our physical and mental condition to varying degrees, depending on our level of interest and sensitivity.

For years I studied and deconstructed the musical coding language of Western Tonal Harmony in search of the lost, buried and forgotten living spiritual wisdom from which our present day understanding of music had descended. Over time I have learned to relax my desire to pin the spirit of music to its harmonic structures. Yet I have also discovered a number of treasure maps in esoteric and occult literature during my research that hinted at the very thing I was initially looking for. In this book, I have attempted to assemble a cohesive narrative that links together all of my favorite magical and philosophical frameworks, with the end goal of re-contextualizing Western music.

The problem with trying to talk about musical meaning and its evocative power could be summarized in the following way; Melodies convey sonic, vibrational, wordless, and trans-ideational metaphors for inner situations. Their evocative power defies the familiar one-to-one mapping of words and definite meanings that we encounter in other verbal languages. Music participates in a much richer kind of mapping of the *many-to-the-many*, linking pure oscillatory organisms of physical sound waves and their movement through space to the emotional layers of our human body-mind. There is more than one translational map of musical meaning between sound and human emotion.

Any time we construct a model of the world, we can be certain that we are omitting information. That being said, the models presented in this book do not claim to be comprehensive. Instead, they are intended to inspire an intuitive relationship to the mysteries of music, guiding our imagination toward new ways of hearing and understanding sound. Additionally, these models may be exploited to compose new music and get in touch with the archetypal forces that influence our daily lives.

Remember that music theory is just a labeling system defined by predetermined grammatical rules. It describes the organization of sound according to emergent laws and tendencies. There is no single, authoritative metaphysical dictionary for translating musical forms into spiritual concepts. It is up to you, the individual, while reading through these contents, to decide whether the worldviews employed substantially contribute to your inner relationship to music.

... Our felt experience of music takes place inwardly and is actually not located in the music at all ...

It has become common knowledge today that music is not located *inside* individual musical notes but rather in our perception of the space between them. These intervals of sound/silence touch something within the human psyche that is, in truth, still very much a mystery. A composer who has made contact with and laid bare some element of his or her own soul through the medium of music cannot help but to extend an influence into the collective mind-sphere, shedding light upon similar elements in the audience's psyche. The artist's rendering of personal psychic content triggers us sympathetically by means of what Jung called the collective unconscious, revealing to us the transpersonal and mythic qualities of our human experience, in some cases raising us to the dramatic heights of initiatory revelation.

Over time, musicians tend to develop ways of listening and playing that are uniquely their own. The models presented in this book are non-dogmatic and represent just a few possible angles that one could take in the art of interpretive and speculative music. It recognizes and relates to, but does not claim to be entirely compatible with, the conventions of Western Tonal Harmony. It does operate within the twelve-tone system of equal temperament, and from this palette one can derive all of the familiar scales and chords that one would expect to hear in American and European music, yet because it borrows from principles of astrology and alchemy, there are a number of other musical structures available through the **Tone Color Alchemy** system that would never occur to someone firmly entrenched in classical Western approaches to music composition.

To unveil the true nature of a song, we need to acknowledge that its component parts express themselves simultaneously through *multiple channels*. Not unlike the astrologer who turns to the stars and planets for symbols of the soul, we can use the methods of Tone Color Alchemy to evaluate the events of our life and formulate meaningful musical representations of them. I would caution against attempting to reverse engineer a piece of music according to this symbolic network. It is intended to stimulate and supplement our natural creative impulses, *encoding* rather than *decoding musical meaning*.

* ENTER AT YOUR OWN RISK *

This book entertains metaphysical ideas as if they were of genuine value to the operator.

ASTROMUSIK has been formulated during a period in history where models of occult musical correspondence have more or less had *fallen out of style*. Professor Joscelyn Godwin composed many of the great books on this topic during the late 1980's and early 1990's, documenting and nurturing the lineage of speculative music with great care and a high degree of academic proficiency. Gary Tomlinson fired back with his book on *Music in Renaissance Magic* around 1994, conducting an equally rigorous evaluation of musical occultism and offering a negative counterpoint to Godwin's optimistic attitudes, accusing him of "New Age Occultism". In a telling moment, somewhere near the end of his book, **Tomlinson states matter-of-factly that the astrological and alchemical mysticism of Renaissance music failed to achieve the practical effects and benefits claimed by its proponents**. This declaration is reminiscent of those moments in a chemistry textbook where alchemical emblems are featured briefly, only to be dismissed as hocus-pocus. In emphasizing the failure of music to accomplish feats of natural magic, Tomlinson summarily sidesteps the treatment of music's psychological and spiritual implications.

There is more musical output today than at any other point in history, but very few people are engaging in deep thought and dialogues about the musical medium itself. A number of questions are waiting to be answered. Why do we divide the octave into twelve notes? Why are there seven notes in a diatonic scale? What is the philosophical taproot of these musical parameters and how can songwriters work to integrate magic back into the composition process?

ASTROMUSIK is designed as an art-piece and a mutation of multiple coinciding influences. The format of this book is partly derivative (see ASTROLOGIK by Berkeley author and filmmaker Antero Alli). The philosophical basis of Tone Color Alchemy borrows heavily from the inner teachings of the Hermetic Order of the Golden Dawn, an infamous branch of Freemasonry with ties to Crowley, Israel Regardie, and Paul Foster Case of the B.O.T.A. Most of the research behind this book was conducted between 2006-2013 as a response to the models of conventional music theory that I took in during my brief foray through university education (MUSIC THEORY I-IV + COUNTERPOINT + EAR TRAINING + PERFORMANCE). It represents a long-term attempt to break free from the shackles of Tonal Harmony, to rediscover the innocence and unassuming musical curiosity I enjoyed during my youth, and to disrobe a lineage of Western esoteric thought that reignited the fire of my own musical creativity over the past decade.

Final Warning: If you don't enjoy exploring the contents of your imagination, please close this book and forget the whole thing.

Acoustic Memetics

Non-Verbal Musical Meaning Structures

Archetypal symbols, including musical themes, can take on a number of different meanings depending on one's personal associations to them. By analogy, someone who spent their childhood playing in the woods may have a pleasant experience of a forest dream, while a city dweller may regard the woods as an unfamiliar and threatening environment. In both scenarios the forest symbol invokes the mysteries of nature, but the life experience of the dreamer changes the meaning of that symbol. In a similar way, a piece of music can mean something different to each person. Personal associations with a musical moment may include thoughts, feelings, memories, and so forth. Our rational mind wants to create logical statements about music in order to understand it, such as "the melody ascends, so I think of moving upward" and "I recognize this as a children's song, I think of children". However, our imagination produces associations that are more analogical and not so directly correlated. It makes no difference what we think of, so long as we're really tuning in to the music and allowing the associations to freely sprout from the mental link between the song and our subconscious mind.

Dreams are a theatre of the soul, where the dreamer takes on the role of playwright, performer, and audience all at once. The creative process of Music composition is similar; songwriters imagine, perform and listen to their songs all at once. Psychic energy rooted in the upper-dimensional domains of Mind appears to the creative artist in a variety of forms, sometimes as a melody or chord progression, while other times it appears as an image, thought, or somatic feeling. The central task of a musician is to translate these seeds of psychic energy into sound frequencies. Every person has his or her own way of arriving at the final musical product, but the initial creative impulse is always a critical starting point.

Human consciousness seems to be composed of at least three important parts; a formless observer, an indwelling spiritual and genetic propensity for certain ways of being, and a socio-cultural programming that sculpts our thoughts and actions according to its customs. Language and musical meaning operate primarily through the third channel, internalized by the individual as a way of relating adequately and appropriately to the collective, our willingness to subscribe to these social codes being informed in a deep way by our animal instincts for survival and pleasure. One of the most fundamental liberties of humankind is to learn how to reprogram the inherited language and conceptual maps of reality so as to discover our *true nature*.

What makes music so unique is its self-referential quality. A musical event can only be understood meaningfully in terms of other intratextual and extratextual musical events. Music rarely refers to specific physical and external things in the world, and when it does we recognize it immediately as an artifice. Songcraft involves, with few exceptions, the ability to portray unnamable and invisible forces through sound.

As a product of Western culture, the language of music is inseparable from our dominant, mentally programmed relationship to trans-cultural archetypes in the collective human psyche. Our task is to understand how meaning (i.e. archetypal energy) is embedded into cultural forms in general. We will presently explore this question through the study of memetics, a relatively young field of scientific inquiry that describes cultural information transference in terms of biological evolutionary tendencies. Analogous to the scientific concept of a gene, the *meme* is described as a unit of culture hosted by human minds, seeking to replicate and transfer its content from one person to the next. Its lifespan is determined by its usefulness within the various socio-cultural matrices to which it belongs. Often times it will glom on to other memetic structures so as to improve its likelihood of survival. In this way, our world's myths and musical masterpieces have taken form beginning with the simplest memetic-thematic devices and building up over time into vast networks of cultural ideology. Our minds behave like complex machines, internalizing these ideas, accepting or rejecting them, storing, utilizing, and even transfiguring them so as to render them useful in our own biological survival. One could argue that memes are also useful for trans-terrestrial psychic circuitry, granting us insights into astral travel and various other disembodied states of consciousness. In other words, memes are not merely applicable to mundane mind states but also to the navigation of advanced spiritual states.

When memes cluster together, they form a new structure whose impact upon consciousness is potentially more nuanced and effective than any of its individual parts. Take for example a musical melody, composed of individual notes that by themselves are modest and unassuming, yet when coupled in a sequence of intervals can produce a musical idea that worms its way into our auditory cortex and doesn't go away. We won't have much luck trying to make sense of the melody in terms of its individual notes, but we can make sense of harmonic interval fragments and their relations to one another, especially if we are clued in to the subtle codes of Western music. Every musical product spawns from a database of culture. Even those musical events that trigger ecstatic, transcendental states can be intellectually traced back to the composer's implementation of special musical and memetic devices.

Transference of memes between human hosts represents the localized expression of a nonlocal, more expansive exchange taking place in the mind sphere, or *ideosphere*. Anyone with access to the cultural schematics of a civilization is theoretically able to exert control over the population through skillful use of its symbols. New memetic structures are assembled to subtly manipulate the subconscious assumptions and beliefs of a people. Typically this is accomplished through the dramatic play of human archetypes and myth in movies and theatrical performances. Music composition plays an integral role in psychic engineering, imbuing the dramatic human archetypes of myth with a deeper harmonic and geometric subtext. In this way, certain types of archetypal events in film and theatre can be consistently linked to musical forms so as to create deep, subconscious associations between the two. The average person passively absorbs their audio-visual indoctrination into a cultural meme sphere without any second thoughts. What most of us don't realize is how the deepest core of our ego-identities are being molded by that culture, instilled with non-universal beliefs and assumptions used by the programmers to remote-control us. Inquiry into musical memetics as a method of social engineering is essential, even if somewhat uncomfortable to accept. Memetic structures can be used both consciously and unconsciously to subtly force an individual into behavioral conformity against their will. Culture-hosts are often indoctrinated into their worldview to such a degree that they cannot understand how anyone else would see the world differently. Encounters with foreign meme-fields can pose a real threat to inflexible ego structures, because like a virus, ideas can easily propagate and take root in the psyche against our will.

As events unfold on our planet, microcosmic musical laws mutate and shape-shift to reflect these changes in the collective. When a meme fails to bind to a host organism, it remains encoded in that physical artifact and may wait indefinitely to be internalized by another entity. If that artifact in question disappears without sufficient sociocultural integration of its indwelling spirit, it runs the risk of extinction. Like Darwin's notion of the *survival of the fittest*, these memes must literally "fit" into our database of cultural significance if they wish to survive. Those ideas that do fit into and modify pre-existing structures of a cultural pod have the power to create corresponding changes in the behavior of its human hosts.

Inasmuch as music influences and organizes the activities of mind, and considering that the way we organize our thoughts influences the actions we take in the world, it follows that music may be exploited to shape consensus reality and its physical manifestations. Adaptive and transformational tendencies within a cultural macrocosm vary depending on the root assumptions of that culture. An operating system whose memetic structure includes the axiom {*novelty creates instability*} is unlikely to generate or relate in a healthy way to microcosmic-harmonic novelty. Commercial music is the best example of this inflexible and calcified attitude towards innovation. Driven by an appeal to the market, corporate executives attempt to identify stable formulas, find musicians who can replicate the formula, and disseminate the product to a target audience with the express intention of capitalizing on their gullibility. From the perspective of musical economics, the audience is little more than a programmable, mind-controlled energy source. By establishing a homogenized meme pool of microcosmic musical codes, these figures can effectively control the perceptions of its audience for long periods of time.

Transmoral to the core, myth has an innate power to sculpt and influence reality in accordance with our consciously activated will. If we're not careful, the blessing power of music and memetic programming can be inverted and turned against us, particularly through a seduction to gain power over others. This has become especially apparent in the black arts of corporate marketing and advertising, a domain where the symbol-illiterate masses are often manipulated into believing that such-and-such a product is going to provide them something essential to human life that in reality it never could and never does. Alert, alert! This kind of manipulative social engineering is where the transmoral essence of myth becomes amoral and can lead the naïve down a dark, soul-destroying path justified by the seemingly common-sense inexorability of the need to make money and maximize corporate profit.

Acoustic physics and professional audio production have never been more advanced. Yet without the blessing of a songwriter's higher genius for harmonic innovation, music can quickly become homogenous and redundant. The lack of adventurous musicianship in the modern world has become a serious issue. Facing the dilemma of modern music, we turn to speculative musicology and can begin to redefine, reinterpret, and reimagine our way into the existing musical forms so as to find new methods of creating and listening. Thankfully, the dross of mainstream music and its ideological fundamentalism repels a substantial number of artists into countercultural and revolutionary attitudes toward the establishment, reflected in their strange deviations from the musical norms.

An individual or subculture operating on the assumption that {*novelty is healthy*} will tend to be more open to mutations in the musical microcosm. Musicians who pledge to make innovations to the medium often struggle immensely against the inertia of conventional musical reality tunnels. Unfortunately, this is the price they pay for individuating from the herd.

In psychological terms, the collective unconscious, as a combined psyche of all human civilizations, holds the records of every existing physical and memetic structure in totality. Languages, including music, represent the psychic circuitry of information exchange, whereby energy is encapsulated, organized and circulated through the collective human psyche to produce physical results. A person who has not learned to disengage from their earliest social programming will remain more or less trapped in that subculture, and in turn, in the modes of behavior deemed appropriate.

Whoever opens up to the infinitude of aesthetic possibilities in the art world as though they were all *potentially* valuable can expect to be transformed by the internal memetic mutations that follow. The apparent antagonism between culture and counter-culture can be dispelled through our awareness of the macrocosm as a holistic social organism of which we are a part. To take sides with one camp exclusively is to lose sight of the big picture and its perfection as a memetic field. It is nearly impossible for us to live without aesthetic biases, but to view and judge the world's music as if our preferences were 'correct' leads to an unnecessarily limited relationship to the world's music. Our judgments upon music are a function of ego identification with a limited cultural program.

Symbols and myth are inherently neutral, neither good nor bad, or perhaps both good *and* bad, depending on how we view it. We are each individually responsible for the way we wield our creative power. An adequate interpretation of symbols requires that we have access to a highly subjective, personalized mythic landscape of meaning and significance. The resulting belief system may be refined and sophisticated or fragmentary and haphazard depending on how much inner work we have put into cultivating our inner life. As we enhance the harmony of our symbolic codes, we infuse both our inward and outward experiences with a wealth of meanings whose richness depends on the architectural integrity of our inner, psychic temple. Our personal myth is charged with personal and collective meaning patterns that orient us like guide posts and inform our free will. This process unfurls moment-by-moment as we navigate through the living dreamscape. In turn, the ways in which we relate to the melodic and harmonic phrasing of a song will vary depending on our relationship to the sociocultural matrix with which we identify.

Music, whose sonic-mythic content reflects both conscious and subconscious contents of the autonomous psyche, is the premier symbolic expression of psychic energy. Following this further, music offers an audible mirror, reflecting internal conditions with a tendency to synchronize and correlate to the source of that very music. Our self-image is a product of the stories we internalize from our cultural informants, whose contents are in turn influenced and informed by the, big-picture mythological archetypes of the world at large. The characters and scenarios of myth are part of our cultural inheritance, the nucleus around which our sense of ego-identity constellates. What we perceive as happening objectively in music is truly a reflection of something happening within us. We are dreaming up the world around us in a way that is informed by both our perceptions and projections. Just as music has the potential to convey a power that transcends the identifiable structures of its audible form, so do words also point to universal and elemental principles cloaked in presuppositions of the culture to which it belongs. The whole of civilization seems to be the result of linguistic influences upon human perception, and the superimposition of these perceptions onto the world at large.

To understand our own musical biases and cultural programming, we need to develop an understanding of how musical meaning is formulated and maintained. There are two distinct, interconnected spheres of memetic influence that we can identify in the field of speculative music. At the most fundamental level, we encounter the archetypal phenomena of the musical tone, the atomic units of music and their bonds to one another as musical harmony. Like molecular clusters, these harmonic groups are arranged in sequence to produce higher orders of harmonic relationship, what we call the *chord progression.* Chord progressions become "units" unto themselves and are juxtaposed against one another, as in the classic ABA' or ABBA structure, to produce song forms. In more elaborate and lengthy musical structures, such as the classical symphony, these same principles of note, interval, and chord progression + melody are still utilized. For the sake of simplicity, we can classify this body of *tonal harmony* as the musical *microcosmos.*

In juxtaposition to the musical microcosm of harmony is the socio-cultural matrix and *musical macrocosm* of genre. Melodic and harmonic forms are granted meaning predominantly by those cultures that inform their genesis. The performance and presentation of music to the audience is equally important. In some cases, the way a person embodies and performs a piece of music is the most meaningful element of that energetic transmission. The images that accompany a piece of music contribute to how we perceive it as well. In reality, there is no part of the musical microcosm that does not owe its effectiveness to the cultural and countercultural biases that both inform and perceive it. Vice versa, there could be no musical culture without the memetic exchange of ideas, and no ideas without the archetypal process of microcosmic musical tone intervals. Musical meaning is hooked into other artistic macrocosms like poetry, film, theatre, and fashion. In these spheres, musical expression is subordinated to the role of cultural signifier, becoming an expendable commodity and placeholder to be traded and monetized in service to the collective, human drama. The outward-oriented domains of artistic culture help to define stable elements of psychological identity among its members. Genres are like sonic territory, the audience its citizens, the microcosmic musical elements its ecological and architectural landscape, the macrocosmic stylistic variations and socio-cultural biases an equivalent to the political arena. The macrocosm informs our collective, creative transmutation of memetic information as reflections of the present day realities of human life.

As intermediary transductors between the macro/micro worlds of culture and musical harmony, our mind-body hologram is being constantly sculpted according to the energies passing through it. Parallel to the metaphysical distinctions of microcosmos and macrocosmos is the distinction of what is *within and without*. Appreciation for musical harmony is a fundamentally inward process, even though the audible signals may come from outside of us. Suggestions from a movie's soundtrack, for example, can link certain characters and narrative situations with musical motifs, establishing an *intraparadigmatic* structure. The predominance of consonance or dissonance may lend to our perception of their role in the story. Their personalities become infused with and inseparable from their musical accompaniment. Richard Wagner called these melodies *leitmotifs*, a German word indicating a "leading motive" or musical theme. The *Lord of the Rings* series, for example, features one of the largest collections ever of recurring leitmotifs, each one representing a recurring character, location, or situation in the film. The audience is coerced into unconscious memetic associations between sound and image, forging an emotional synergy between psyche, music, and myth.

Theatre may also draw upon *extratextual* paradigms of music, such that the perceived meaning of a scene is informed not by the composer's use of recurring themes within that film, but by the long term, cumulative impact of a psychic relationship between audience and conventions of tonal harmony within the parameters of a certain culture or set of cultures. Imagine a movie scene where the composer has paired classical music with the imagery of a prestigious ballroom party. The film score in this example draws upon our cultural associations between a style of music and its native culture, inciting an emotional response based on our subjective interpretation of these extratextual associations. Encoded into all extratextual music is a self-contained musical microcosm, i.e. the song itself, whose subtleties of internal meaning may or may not have any noticeable impact upon our experience of the movie or theatrical performance. Instead, these sounds are used as cultural signifiers and associative cues for the creation of cinematic moods and atmosphere.

A primary goal of speculative music is to dissolve the boundary between extratextual and intratextual frameworks, to realize the underlying, unified dream-field of our collective imagination. Each of us, as composers and audience, are participatory observers in a **Mass Shared Dream.** Surrendering to knowledge of the interdependence of all the world's activity is not merely a passive act. We are being called forward to engage the dream directly and with skillful means. Knowledge of music theory sharpens the sword of the intellect and grants us a finely tuned appreciation of music's transcendental properties. The cross-disciplinary studies of music and myth will prove equally useful to students of astrology, alchemy, magic, and psychology, as all of these fields of study deal with symbolic representations of our inner life. Investigations into the deeper field dynamics of consciousness result in heightened creativity and lucidity, the energies most responsible for maintaining our sense of happiness and wellness as human beings. Stationed at the center of these micro-macro and intra-extratextual worlds of music is our treasured human individual, the anthropic principle, the nervous system sensorium and transmitter-receiver vessel without which none of this would be possible. In perceiving the musical microcosm, our bodies subconsciously internalize and integrate unfathomable quantities of sonic information to produce simple intuitive responses of appreciation or disapproval. Depending on our macrocosmic informants, the cultural operating systems driving and sustaining our ego-identity, we can get in touch with a variety of internal, emotional and psychological responses.

Appreciation for musical harmony is a fundamentally inward process, even though the audible signals may come from outside of us. Through listening and processing, the inner world of the psyche potentially develops and produces a coherent response to the music. Creative and embodied responses to sound represent an outward flow from our inner process to the world at large. By stepping into an active, creative role as the artist-shaman-healer, we can join consciously in the processes of memetic mutation and give birth to new musical entities. Liberating ourselves from the cultural inheritance of our nuclear and extended family, we can branch out and explore new domains of the imagination, arriving at an individual aesthetic pallet that allows for conscious synthesis of the memetic codes of our choice. In birthing new musical forms, we become the caretakers and stewards of that memetic mutation. Creative artists explore this invisible landscape of the imagination and enjoy the unique privilege of restructuring it in whatever way they please.

The role of the artist and musician is not only one of microcosmic engineering, but also of social networking and memetic propagation. When new memes are formulated in an individual's mind and then released into the collective ideosphere by way of art, they take on a life of their own, jumping from one host to the next and binding to the receptive edges of compatible memetic structures. Their goal seems to be the creation of increasingly complex mental and cultural entities. If they fail to bind and replicate through pre-existing structures, these memes have nowhere to go and will dissolve back into the mental ether. This survival impetus creates the incentive for aggressive, memetic self-propagation. An unfathomably rich tapestry of memetic programming underlies the ego-identities of all human culture, including but not limited to Western civilization. When memetic structures become sufficiently robust, it is as if they develop an archetypal power or spiritual body that is imbued with what we would typically call *consciousness*. These memetic spirits, having a life of their own, operate through the mind and in the case of larval states of human consciousness may even be largely responsible for directing an individual's actions according to their own whims.

Once released into the collective psyche, these spiritual artifacts take on an autonomous existence, binding to the receptive inlets of other people's established memetic structures. Like a virus, the meme is aggressively self-interested and potentially infiltrates the subconscious, whether we like it or not. The degree of change it exerts upon our worldview depends upon its own nature and the flexibility of our dominant socio-cultural biases. In less negative terms, the meme is an effective way of shifting an individual's psycho-spiritual disposition toward a more desirable state of being, and the musical theme represents the conjunct application of musical and mythic memetics to the healing arts.

Choosing **the blessing way**, we can nurture those blueprints that spell happiness and personal growth for all sentient beings. Deviations from the intention of support and empowerment can generate negative karma that manifests in unstable states of mind and distress, a warping of our connection to the precious and sacred source of our creativity, leading to internal confusion, anxiety, and suffering, not to mention the witless undermining and destruction of our precious open-ended human potential. Thus the best way to defeat our enemies, as taught by all the wisdom traditions, is to generate compassion and unconditional love, coupled with the strength to protect oneself from their negative influences.

This translates musically as the appropriate use of dissonance in relation to consonance, and mythically/astrologically, as the willingness to locate the gifts inherent in our most challenging personal planetary and zodiacal configurations. Furthermore, it means a relativistic model of the cosmos, where the forces of good and evil hang in the balance, neither one exerting inordinate power over the other. All forms are ultimately empty and devoid of intrinsic meaning, but relative to one another and in relationship to an attentive, sensitive human mind, they acquire an abundance of individualized meaning. It is as if our task in life is to uncover, explore, and integrate as many qualitatively different states of being as we see fit in our search for and attainment of happiness. We thereby endlessly, actively explore the boundless frontier of musical harmony as a microcosmic harmonization with divine, cosmic order and the totality of existence. This exploration when wisely conducted opens up our infinite, yet so often barely tapped, capacities for delight, bliss, joy and fulfillment, all of which by their very nature serve to bring us more and more into phase with our innate, infinite intelligence.

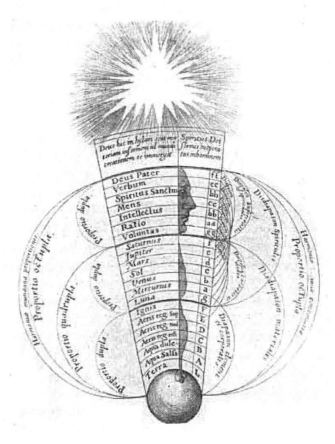

The Castle of Knowledge; Robert Recorde, 1556

The Disenchanted World of Absolute Music

Western music began its transition from the Baroque and Classical eras to the Romantic period of music around the turn of the 19th century. Generally speaking, the composers of the Romantic era defined themselves in opposition to the Industrial Revolution, rejecting the suffocative, mechanistic, intellectual conventions that had emerged during the so-called "Age of Enlightenment". Romantic music emphasized the mysteries of Nature in their musical moods and deviated from the musical formulas of their predecessors, experimenting with chord types and song structures that had not yet been explored. Despite their opposition to the industrial and mechanical worldviews, composers benefited from these technological developments, gaining access to improved musical instruments available at lower costs. As the middle class began to swell, more people could afford to participate in music, including the purchasing of instruments and the leisure to spend time working on their performance. Mental and emotional attitudes that previously had been marginalized, due to Western composers' dependence upon aristocratic benefactors, began to percolate up to the surface of musical culture, impacting and reconfiguring consensus reality.

A philosophical current called "Absolutism" influenced the aesthetics of Romantic era music in a big way, promoting the attitude that music had no meaning whatsoever and that our enjoyment of it was purely a function of the way that it articulates passages through empty forms. They believed that no extra-musical contents were necessary for the music to have an impact, and in fact, most composers argued that attributing concepts to music only *detracted* from its absolute purity. German music critic Eduard Hanslick famously remarked, "Music has no subject beyond the combinations of notes we hear, for music speaks not only by means of sounds, it speaks nothing but sound." In other words, absolute music was considered by its proponents to be complete unto itself, its highest virtue defined by its intrinsic dissociation from all sense of worldly purpose.

The Romantic composers' had a genuine appreciation for nature and the Mysteries, but their worldview did not represent a return to the Neo-Platonic magic of the Renaissance period. On the contrary, the idea that musical notes *actually* correlated to planetary spheres was antithetical to the Absolutists. Professor Daniel Chua wrote one of the best books on this subject, entitled *"Absolute Music and the Construction of Meaning"*, in which he describes the philosophical tenets and problems of Absolute music in great detail. According to Chua, the central schism between Modern music and the mystical sentiment of ancient Greek musical philosophy happened when we began using 12-tone equal temperament for the tuning of our instruments. An equal subdivision of the octave represented the Western world's desire to intellectually chop up and categorize the Mysteries, gaining control over music while at the same time bringing us dangerously close to disenchantment. The age of Enlightenment aimed to dominate the unknown by reducing our *feelings* to quantifiable *facts*.

The 18th century (known as the Age of Enlightenment) promised to banish all ghouls and phantoms from the Western imagination and replace them with clean machines. Modern man believed he was immune to any belief in God because the cycles of nature that previously frightened him were now objectified and demystified - perhaps erratic in their behavior but no longer an expression of God's transcendent will. Invisible forces no longer dressed themselves up in the costume of fairies and demons. Chua cites a quote from the German sociologist Max Weber, "The fate of an epoch which has eaten of the tree of knowledge is that it must know that *it cannot learn the meaning of the world from the result of its analysis*". How true this is of music, which prior to twelve-tone equal temperament presented musical tones as a direct transmission from the *Harmony of the Spheres*.

Mechanization of music, both in the building of equally tempered instruments and in its strict methods of composition, spelled the death of Pythagorean tuning methods, and therefore a blockade to humankind's immersion in the Pythagorean mysteries. The ancient Greek philosophers used simple whole number ratios to tune their instruments. They also demonstrated how spatial intervals between planets in our solar system were built upon the very same whole number integers. Thus, they proposed that music brought the subtle energies of heaven down to Earth. Research into the history of Western instrumental tuning methods reveals that the twelve-tone system utilized in all standard instruments today represented a deviation from the Pythagorean worldview. Chopping up the circle into equal parts produced intervals that were harmonically out of phase but intellectually "useful". The Western mind was involuntarily subjected to a shift away from melodic enchantment. New harmonic progressions were artificial, an expression of human will and intellectualism rather than the pre-existent posture of intuitive song, humility and whole-hearted surrender to the mysterious forces of Nature.

Western music is literally out of tune with what modern science calls the *harmonic overtone series*. The insufficiency of equal temperament is not merely a new-age value judgment, but a scientific and acoustic *fact*. Sound frequencies in nature begin with what is called a fundamental tone, or sound frequency, similar to the sine wave described in previous chapters of this book. Unlike the sine wave, which is mathematically abstracted from nature – a monotonic frequency devoid of overtones - naturally occurring fundamental tones feature a harmonic overtone series sound that hover above the fundamental and express barely audible pitches in special interval relationships. An instrument's tone quality, or timbre, is largely determined by the materials used in the building of the instrument, which cause the volume levels of each overtone in the series to vary.

A single vibrating string, prior to any division into semitones, expresses a harmonic overtone series whose intervals are in fact the basis of our modern 12-Tone Equal Temperament system. From the root note (fundamental tone), it builds vertically with overtones of an octave, followed by a perfect fifth interval, then a perfect fourth, then a major third, a minor third, and so forth, ascending in increasingly smaller ratios. However, the harmonic intervals that we call a "perfect fifth", "perfect fourth", and "major and minor third" in the language of Western tonality are all harmonically imperfect, due to our manipulation of the ratios that naturally emerge from the actual harmonic overtone series of an open string. Applying 12-tone equal temperament to the tuning of an instrument is like putting braces on the seemingly crooked teeth of a child in order to "straighten them out". Invasive and unnatural, yet capable of producing results, equal temperament bends nature into submission so as to achieve an aesthetic that it deems appropriate and good.

In a later chapter on Near Death Experiences, I cite research that demonstrates how artificially induced Out of Body Experiences tend to attract situations where an individual's disembodied consciousness hears *instrumental* music, whereas natural death incidents tend to attract *vocal* music instead. This speaks to the idea that, even in the case of harmonically in-phase instruments like those of the Ancient Greeks, the human voice is closer to our true nature than musical instruments, which are the direct result of our applied mental reasoning power. The equal temperament of instruments that emerged during the age of Enlightenment embodied a larger cultural pattern of dissociation from metaphysical gnosis that previously informed the music of the West.

Vincenzo Galilei conducted a number of experiments during the late 16th century that attempted to demonstrate empirically the physical laws of sound. In contrast to those who had come before him, Galilei viewed music as if it were a wholly material phenomenon, devoid of any magical properties. The materials used in the building of an instrument were seen to be always variable and therefore imperfect. In contrast to the perfect and immutable forms of the Pythagorean dream, the new acoustic worldview would concern itself with endless calculations of the material domain, taking note of its constant nuances so as to create the ideal instrumental machine, while simultaneously thrusting a dagger into the heart of Mystery. All that had been previously left to the imagination was now projected onto the "outside world" and measured. Whatever projections could not be measured physically were considered irrelevant and non-existent. Thus not only nature and its harmonic overtone series, but also the surreal and phantasmal quality of the imagination itself, became systematically quashed and overturned by Reason.

As one would expect, the demystification of tone and harmony had an irreversible impact on Western music over the following centuries. Vincenzo's musical compositions were not tributes to the mysteries of Heaven. They were demonstrations of his twisted instrumental logic, mechanical and heartless, built upon the assumption that sound is nothing more than physical vibrations through air and an equally physical perception of sound via the human body. The human body itself had been intellectually reduced to a kind of soulless machine.

Platonic and Pythagorean musical philosophy brought together seemingly disparate elements of life in harmony with one another, indicating a divine order behind the creation and sustenance of the Universe. Equal temperament rejected this worldview in favor of pragmatic understanding of things "as they actually are". Chuo demonstrates in his book how the 19th century romantic composers attempted to re-enchant the world through the development of an Absolute Music. Rather than rejecting equal temperament and returning to Pythagorean methods, the Romantics attempted to integrate modern tuning methods in the construction of a new domain of meaning, an "extra-musical" space that would exist as interdependent and yet distinct from the physical sounds. According to Chuo, however, the Romantics failed to accomplish this task. The anti-metaphysical assumptions of 12-TET were so deeply ingrained and had so thoroughly traumatized our sense of mystery, both philosophically and acoustically, that the Romantic notion of absolute music amounted to a kind of spiritual escapism, an attempt to project our lost-object, the sunken Atlantis of early musical mystery, onto the barren imaginal landscape of modern tonal harmony.

According to the philosophy of Absolute Music, the instrumental tuning methods of modernity were not inherently problematic. Instead, our reduction of "pure music" to its physical counterparts was the problem. Therefore music was put on a pedestal and worshipped as if it were God itself, representing an inner reality of secular mystical initiation. The composer and audience affectations were triggered by the transcendental object of music, its emptiness and meaninglessness interpreted as its highest virtue. Chuo suggests that this attitude, far from being a return to an Edenic paradise, was actually a sad cover story for the creeping sense of nihilism that had emerged during the Age of Reason.

Western culture's departure from philosophical unity with the celestial harmony of the spheres had serious consequences. Our sense of wonder vanished with Copernican attitudes toward the solar system, and with it, so too did our soul's connection to the Monocosm. The idea of *having a life purpose* was drastically altered. Music transitioned from being a means of offering sacred invocations and incantations to Spirit, toward a fabricated, artificial and intellectual collection of theories about our newly founded harmonic science. Consequently, our cultural attitudes toward the mystery of nature simultaneously shifted into the commodification of "objects" for personal gain and sensual gratification. Like a war veteran speculating endlessly about their phantom limb, Romanticism made a valiant effort to solve the crisis of meaninglessness in modern culture by theorizing about the emptiness between musical notes. Sadly, their theories only made more obvious the culture's psychological split between musical tones and their vanishing spirituality.

Many world cultures are without a word for music, despite the central role played by sacred song in the rites and ceremonies of their people. Anthropologists have attributed the undifferentiated interconnectivity of art, poetry, dance and music in these traditions to their preoccupation with animistic and unscientific worldviews. In our own Western culture, music has been so completely abstracted from its original condition that it seems ludicrous to talk about a tone as having any intrinsic "meaning". Conversely, primitive musical expressions are so full of meaning that they express the opposite polarity – they don't view music as being separate from the things that it apparently signifies. From one perspective, the Western cultural dissociation from en-spirited musical tones seems tragic. It mirrors a similar body-mind split happening in our culture. Yet from another view, this split may actually be a necessary precursor to evolution in the consciousness of our species. Divorcing music from its natural order in the cosmos and objectifying it as a physical phenomenon serves the magical purpose of **banishing superstition**.

Ceremonial magic of the west, especially from the 19th century onward, regards the **banishing ritual** as an essential preliminary step to the higher degrees of initiation into the Mysteries. The Lesser Banishing Ritual of the Pentagram (LBRP) promoted by the Hermetic Order of the Golden Dawn, draws upon a combination of embodied movement, prayer and words of power to clear the energy of a space in preparation for deeper states of meditation and magical work. Like the LBRP, the scientific de-magification and disenchantment of the world could be interpreted as a powerful banishing spell, leveling the spiritual playing field to make room for new ways of being that may had previously been deemed heretical. Deeply ingrained cultural taboos, differing from one tribe to the next, are relativized by the power of our disbelief in them.

Like the magician's banishing ritual, absolute music imagined that it could sever all ties between music and the world so as to create a space of pure musical expression. The image of a conductor waving his magic wand at the orchestra became a symbol of the supremacy of the human Ego, dictating the harmony of the spheres from his podium without actually performing upon any musical instruments himself. The instruments of the orchestra are all tuned to 12-Tone Equal Temperament, creating a sense of distance in the audience from the natural harmonic overtone series of Earth, along with a feeling that "everything is under control" by the human will.

Even the most far-out orchestral performances amount to artificial representations of real musical magic, signifying and inviting altered states of consciousness without asking the audience to fully surrender to the natural harmonic order of our planet and the states of consciousness they would evoke. Safe in their cushioned auditorium seats, individuals passively absorb the performance like an omnipotent deity, watching but not participating in the music. This is precisely the attitude promoted by classical physics, which believes that the act of observation has absolutely zero effect upon the experiment at hand. Yet the human race is *not* separate from Earth. Our separateness is merely a sleight of mind, a magic trick of mental perception that only *appears* to create separation.

The postmodern discovery of physics and humanity's quantum interdependence with the world poses an interesting question with respect to the field of speculative music. By and large, people no longer believe that the stars and planets *literally* embody the states of consciousness that they signified in astrology, nor do people believe that chemical elements express the subtle spiritual essences that they did in ancient alchemical art. Similarly, it may seem absurd that a certain musical frequency would be literally connected to astrological and alchemical essences, as the Neo-Platonic tradition of magic would have us believe. Yet to dispense of these magical practices amounts to throwing out the baby with the bathwater. The rich symbolic network of sympathetic correspondence modeled and practiced by the initiates of Western ceremonial magic invite us back to a long lost way of relating to the world.

Like training wheels on a bicycle, ceremonial magic teaches us a method of relating our inner spiritual and psychic life to events in the world through both causal and acausal-synchronistic modes of awareness. **Model Agnosticism**, a term coined by Robert Anton Wilson, reveals the relativity and non-absolute condition of all models of reality, representing in my opinion the crowning jewel of Western occult thought in the 20th century. Wilson's worldview is not one of agnosticism (or antagonism) toward God but rather toward the images and maps we make of God. One can use certain maps and models of reality to attract profound, mind-blowing spiritual experiences through which they come to know the same mysterious presence in the universe that was known to our ancestors, without ever "believing" that this useful model is actually "true" in some kind of absolute sense.

When we let go of our attachment to a pet belief system, we might discover that we can make use of it without being vulnerable to attack from others. Religious wars have all been sourced in one group of people believing in their own B.S. so fully that they become willing to kill anyone who doesn't subscribe to the same model of reality. In some ways, religious dogmatism is precisely what the scientific method has been fighting against, although a person could easily demonstrate how science has fallen into the same trap through its dogmatic physical-materialistic view of the universe. The ability to skillfully hold multiple contradictory and paradoxical worldviews in one's mind without picking sides seems to me to be a sign of higher intelligence. As pure awareness, we can navigate any number of incompatible different perspectives without getting bogged down in trying to defend one against the other.

TONES NOTES STONE

The shapes and textures of music are like passwords. The very act of listening to certain pieces of music can trigger a **Positive User ID** and **Access-Approval** to areas of the psyche that we didn't even know existed. Music theory today resembles a computer programming language with code sequences that produce tangible effects. Tonal harmony in the Western canon amounts to a deeply encoded, sonic structure finding multi-iterative expressions through the familiar interface of song. These deep structures trigger an emotional and psychological response in audiences. We know for example that the image of a beautiful woman on a computer screen is not actually a beautiful woman - merely a symbolic representation of one. In a similar way, music is an artifice haunted by the phantoms of our own mental projections. The energies we encounter when listening to music are none other than our own internal energy.

ASTROMUSIK chronicles hidden elements of Western Music's mystical inheritance and lays out a working model for musical praxis: **TONE COLOR ALCHEMY.** I have never encountered a system like the one proposed in this book; that is precisely what inspired me to assemble it and seek out the right names for its most fundamental categories. After some contemplation, I settled on the anagrammatic series of key terms: **TONES, NOTES, and STONE** because of their ontological interdependence with one another. Literally quantum-entangled, the wave-form of a **tone** and the atomic-form of a **note** are pointing at the same thing through two different lenses.

The way we choose to think about sound will determine the perspectives and conclusions we draw from it. Note/Tone frequencies circulate through the world and consequently transform it. The metaphoric power of music upon the world is mirrored by the alchemical image of the Philosopher's Stone. For the purposes of this book, the **Stone** category will hereafter refer to what famed Renaissance magician Henry Cornelius Agrippa called *Natural* and *Ritual* magic.

Notes correspond to our intellectual ideas *about* sound. They represent the grammar of music and are the things that we write down on staff paper. In contrast, **Tones** deal with actual vibratory frequencies, independent of our theoretical musical overlays upon them. Talking about tones can be tricky, because by definition they are inseparable from the **Stone** category. Tones don't exist separate from their natural environment. They both come from and move through a given space. However, for the sake of simplicity, we will talk about tone frequencies as autonomous entities, distinguishing them from their effects upon the environment.

THE SONIC MONOCOSM: Where Macro Meets Micro
via the strange loop of eternally recurrent cosmogenesis

A single primordial and vibrational essence extends out from silence into materialization through self-ordering and oscillatory organisms of sonic pressure waves. These waves intersect and interact with a finely tuned, balanced, integrated and receptive human body-mind to produce the vivid auditory experiences we call music. Our human sensorium cascades and coherently inter-resonates through multiple layers of the deep structures of *psyche* to breach the ego threshold and complete its boomerang back to Self, that primordial ground of radiant sentience which is the root source of all known phenomena. When this deep layer of Self bears witness to and "hears" the myriad vibrating patterns and oscillatory forms of musical sound, it rumbles with a deep pleasure that echoes through our physical human form as the grace waves of musical ecstasy. The One who hears music is at the same time human and god, delighting in its true nature as sound, becoming self-aware only through its bio-crystalline mirror, the body.

Our capacity to *listen* enables the all-pervasive, formless sentience that takes the form of "us" to experience and enjoy the perfection of its own vibratory emanations. Coupled with our capacity to receive and experience sound through our body is the twin ability to create and produce sound, most notably with our voice. The resonant capacitor of our human form resembles both a stringed and wind instrument. Its vocal chords are animated by respiration, amplified by the cavern of our mouth, and projected outward into the world as sound. The creative thoughts of our divine will find expression through voice and send ripples of psychoacoustic energy out into the field at large.

Music would be impossible without its first cause, the singularity of an original tone whose pure vibration makes the relativity of harmony possible. Each musical element in a song presents an opportunity for the listener to tune into something unknown and of vital importance to their character. Hearing a piece of music and feeling emotionally moved is like having a waking dream, where something deep within us comes forth *from* our imagination and at the same time triggers a response *in* the imagination. Layer upon layer of spiritual agencies fold in upon one another to produce the multi-textural compositions that are our modern, musical inheritance. The *many-to-many* model of musical meaning allows that a musical event may have multiple correlative events, ranging anywhere from physical-material to psycho-spiritual analogs, and that each of these "meanings" can potentially reveal some aspect of the music's spirit while at the same time remaining conceptually limited and therefore incomplete as representations of the root musical metaphor of unity-consciousness.

Audible and Inaudible Tones (Sound Frequencies)

The twelve tones of our modern musical tuning system share at least one thing in common: their sound-body is defined by pitch frequencies, typically measured in terms of cycles per second (Hz). According to the conventions of acoustic physics, vibrating objects like a tuning fork, bell, or human vocal chords are the physical source of all sound waves. The vibration of the physical source disturbs surrounding media, such as air or water, setting it into motion in fluctuating cycles. These oscillatory cycles project omnidirectionally as a spherical pressure wave, the continuity of its compressions and rarefactions totally dependent upon the source vibrations of a physical object.

This scientific model of acoustics clearly has merit, evidenced by its broad practical and technological applications in the "real world" of audible sound frequencies. However, it contains some hidden assumptions that could easily be overlooked. When we view matter in terms of particles, it makes sense to speak of objects as a conglomerate of atomic and elemental building blocks. A tuning fork, for example, is sent into vibratory motion by some initial, physical cause and consequently, pressure waves ripple out through the surrounding environment to be perceived as sound by those with ears to hear. However, according to the laws of quantum mechanics, matter can be considered both a particle and wave, depending on our perspective. If we view matter itself as composed of waves, whose apparent density is merely an illusory projection of the mind, then the standard model of acoustics begins to crumble and we discover the true waviness of the Universe.

According to the quantum wave model, it makes no sense to talk about objects as physically existing separate from our perception of them as such. Particles are most accurately described through models of standing waveforms and matrices of probability. Through this lens, scientists are forced to confront a collection of waves acting upon other waves, generating more waves, all perceived by the mysterious principle of human consciousness. We cannot speak of human consciousness separate from the human nervous system, whose physicality is subject to the very same wave situation. **The whole damn spectacle is waving back at us -- even our own body.** This would suggest that our mental projections of form and physicality onto quantum wave-functions are highly subjective.

Everything Vibrates: The World is a Song

Q.E.D.

Musical Notes and their Celestial Counterparts

The artist-alchemists of Renaissance Europe experimented with chemicals in laboratories, developing a symbolic language to map the first principles of chemistry. From the modern chemist's perspective, alchemists' observations were critically flawed due to experimental contamination with their subjective, psychic contents. Much effort was been made on the part of Science to differentiate the observer from the experiment, to produce the most universally applicable statements about chemical behavior and a language whose definition-of-terms everyone in the field could agree upon.

Carl Jung regarded the symbolic language of alchemy in a different manner. For Jung, alchemical thought served the secret purpose of identifying, processing, and transmuting inner psychic situations through the outer-correlate of chemistry. Along these lines, the subject's influence upon the experiment was not only non-problematic; it was essential! Most alchemists doubled as astrologers, synchronizing their laboratory trials with phases of the moon, seasonal changes, and even subtler planetary rhythms. Drawing from the Platonic and Neo-Platonic traditions, the ordering principle of both the macro-celestial and micro-elemental worlds was considered to be fundamentally mathematical, and it was the special task of music to reveal the principles of astral and alchemical harmony through the medium of sound. With the aid of music, Renaissance alchemists could translate and ultimately listen to their experimental procedures. As their chemical and astronomical maps became increasingly sophisticated and nuanced, so too did their musical systems, giving way to a variety of instrument tunings and musical scales whose logic was derivative of observations made in the astrochemical domains.

Developing sheet music notation made it easier to delineate chord types and chord progressions, empowering alchemists to communicate precisely about the way individual notes were triggering their imagination. This system allowed them to develop a spiritual practice of listening that combined the subjective experience of music with the objective awareness of its harmonic form.

It is no coincidence that our earliest models of Twelve-Tone Equal Temperament - the tuning system used today for all standard instruments, came through **Vincenzo Galilei,** father of the Italian Renaissance astronomer Galileo Galilei. Vincenzo lived during the mid-16th century as a composer and luthier. A builder of musical instruments, he divided the octave as if it were an astrological wheel and was among the first to compose a song in each of the 12 keys.

Music as the Philosopher's Stone

Speculative philosophers through the ages have wondered what the effect of different scales and chords might have upon the human organism and the world at large. For example, the Greek mathematician and philosopher Pythagoras concocted medicines with the aid of musical modes. He experimented with the relationship between scales and planetary frequencies, positing that because the interval sequence from one scalar mode to the next was non-identical, each mode would produce a unique psycho-spiritual effect upon the listener. Studying these effects in detail, he formulated a body of work that identified "*apparatus and contrectations*", a phrase used by one of his biographers, Iamblichus, to describe the utilization of diatonic, chromatic, and enharmonic melodies to reverse the "passions of the soul" and those emotions that cause a person to act against their own better judgment.

Without our knowing it, music re-assembles and circulates the energies of our psychic field in ways that can be either destructive or creative. Henri Cornelius Agrippa, a major proponent of Hermetic-Cabalistic magic during the early 16th century Renaissance period, believed that if we could say with confidence that the four liquid elements of our body were sympathetic to different musical intervals and modes, we would have discovered a physical correlate to the mysterious, spiritual effects of song upon the human being. Agrippa's studies into music mysticism included Franchino Gafori's research into these modes and their sympathy to certain planets and muses. Here again we find an example of speculative music in the Renaissance where something concrete, in this case the planets, are cited as influences upon the musical logos. It harkens back to the Platonic idea of a harmony of the spheres and the anchoring of those harmonic frequencies into the human body by means of physically perceived sound intervals.

Agrippa published a book in 1518 entitled *De Occulta*, featuring a chapter "On the Conformity of Sounds and Songs to the Heavens, and Which Sounds and Songs Correspond to Particular Stars". Borrowing from contemporary Renaissance philosopher Ramos de Pareia, Agrippa identified four *authentic musical modes* that could be used to move the four bodily humors of phlegm, black bile, blood, and yellow bile. A person's emotional attitude was viewed as being directly related to the balance or imbalance of these bodily fluids, while music was depicted as a method of circulating the humors through the body in a way that could shift how somebody felt. Complimenting these four authentic modes were the *plagal musical modes*, which exerted an opposite influence from the authentic modes. Together, the authentic and plagal modes were theoretically capable of altering one's inner chemistry through their work on the four elements.

Katzenklavier; La Nature, 1883

According to the perspective of sympathetic magic, each instrument is ruled by a spirit and could hypothetically transfigure the psychic attitude of a person in accordance with its own nature. A trumpet sounding a triumphant melody would both evoke and invoke the presence of Mars, God of War, the planetary soul most sympathetic to that type of musical expression. Trumpet music was traditionally sounded during battle to placate the human fear of death and activate the fearless, indwelling god of combat.

Wind instruments like the pipe and flute were attributed to the muses and to the nature deity Pan, whose mischievous spirit was embodied in early Greek culture by the intoxicated, wandering, and masked pipers of the city. A stringed instrument resembling a harp, called the lyre, was allegedly conceived of and developed by the gods Hermes and Apollo. Pythagoras was especially fond of the lyre because of its affiliation with Apollo, God of Light, whereas he scorned the earthy nature of windpipes, claiming that they stirred the passions of the body and belonged to theatrical performances rather than musical medicine.

Pythagoras considered the human voice to be the supreme musical instrument, its form and function closely resembling the archetypal image of a Magic Flute.

"After we destroyed the dinosaurs, we stretched their gizzards across the Grand Canyon and invented music." – GWAR (From a 1990 interview with Joan Rivers)

The Root Myth of Astrology and Music

HARMONY OF THE SPHERES

Of the many symbolic languages that potentially correlate to music, astrology has been the most historically prevalent idiom. Many structural similarities between music and astrology will be highlighted over the course of this book. Ceremonial Magicians have long entertained a musical view of heaven and a heavenly view of music.

A long-term process of archetypal codification took place historically as humanity accumulated cultural projections onto its musical intervals. In the imagination of the Platonic and Neo-Platonic philosophers, Stellar constellations resembled primordial clusters of musical notes upon the ledger lines of galactic orbit, moving perpetually along the surface of our celestial sphere - each star humming with a unique frequency of light that tickled the human psyche in its own special way, eliciting and attracting deep mythic content. Each point of starlight exuded a unique sonic vibration akin to the ringing of a bell. Each cluster of stars was bound to the others, perceived by stargazers in geometric form and rendered as a perfect inkblot for the free play of imagination, so that constellations themselves may be understood as musical chords. Vice versa, our formulated laws of musical harmony serve as a microcosmic reminder of the intergalactic Logos.

Geometry is *the* root language of music and astronomy. Astrology represents humanity's collective effort to bridge the gap between astral movements and daily human life by means of visual and narrative imagery, whereas music aims to accomplish the same thing by means of geometric proportions of sound. Early observations of whole number ratios revealed an indwelling cosmic rhythm, a mystery of universal law that appeared in the interval patterns of both music and astral bodies relative to earth. Extending gracefully into the art of myth and music as a structural constant, this ordering principle of the cosmos, or *Logos*, expressed a harmony between its parts that seems to be responsible for the stability and efficacy of the corresponding cultural myths. The pristine principles of mathematics are a scaffold and skeletal structure serving as the common ground between myth and music.

Proof of the connection between star and song can be pinned to the Greek concept of a *harmony of the spheres*. Plato's famous book, *The Republic*, featured a legend called the *Myth of Er* in which the main character dies in battle and witnesses a world of spiritual activity. Souls travel between earth and heaven, some ascending through the sky and others descending to the subterranean bowels of earth as penalty for their wicked deeds in life. Those who had the privilege to leave earth were brought to a meadow, introduced to a pillar of brilliant rainbow light, and received initiation into the spheres of heaven. Depicted as nested circles around the central core of earth and representing symbolically the orbital patterns of each planet, each orbital circle was circumscribed by a siren[1] who sat upon it and was "carried around, uttering a single sound on one pitch ... the whole of them, being eight, composed a single harmony."[2] In this story, the sirens do not merely represent their physical correlates - the planets of our solar system. Embodying an archetypal power, each planet's vibrational transmission was understood to communicate a unique soul frequency that could be experienced symphonically during the soul's journey through its layers.

Stories about the harmony of the spheres are dreamlike and mythical. They do not depict a cold, intellectual, and mathematical realm of abstraction, in the way that our modern field of acoustics and music theory often do. Indeed, the early philosophers considered their system of numbers to be a language originated by a transcendental mind whose creative powers gave rise to the manifest cosmos. From the Greek perspective, human beings were endowed with the power of reason so as to realize and bring to earth these ordering principles of the macrocosm and microcosm. One way the Greeks applied this belief was through a study of ratios between the planets and stars as applied to music.

A third century Roman named Censorinus articulated the common ancestry between music, planets, stars and the soul in his essay "Harmony and Embryology"[3]. Teaching that the human soul is divine and enters our body during the gestation and birth phase of incarnation, Censorinus proposed that our journey of descent through the spheres of heaven prior to arriving on earth was the reason for our appreciation of musical harmony. Furthermore, he gave credit to the immortal gods for our appreciation of certain instruments and the moods they produced. Since the gods were understood to be indwelling, higher-dimensional principles operating at the deep and unseen levels of our collective psyche, it followed that they could be appeased through the medium of our own, individual perceptions.

---

[1] In Greek mythology, the sirens are portrayed as beautiful creatures and daughters of the river god Achelous, who sang otherworldly songs and lured nearby sailors toward the rocky coasts of their island, typically leading to shipwreck and death.

[2] Plato's Republic, *Myth of Er*

[3] This essay was translated and presented by Joscelyn Godwin in his excellent anthology of speculative music, *"Music, Mysticism, and Magic"*.

Marcus Cicero's character Scipio describes the revolution of heavenly spheres as being so swift and intense that human ears could not "capture" it, suggesting the double meaning of not being able to hear the spheres with our mundane organs of perception and being incapable of capturing this heavenly music with worldly instruments. We might as well stare at the sun directly, suggested Cicero, for the song of these planetary souls would overwhelm our ears the way solar rays do human eyes. Similar reports have emerged in modern times through research into paranormal psychology and Out of Body Experiences (OBEs). Encounters with death are often accompanied by the sound of beautiful, otherworldly music.

Research into the field of paranormal psychology has turned up some remarkable discoveries regarding the role of music in humankind's near-death and out of body experiences. In studying the relationship between music and NDE/OBE as detailed in clinical case studies, we can develop an appreciation for the universality of astral music - not merely as a relic of ancient metaphysical storytelling, but rather as an actual tendency of perception during the moment of death. Psychologists and scientists have catalogued a great many examples of such events over the years. For example, the journalist and research scientist D. Scott Rogo presents an anthology of such incidents in his book *Casebook of Otherworldly Music*. Rogo's research offers a combination of primary source documents and personal commentary, in order to propose a number of theoretical models that may explain what occurs when people have this kind of experience. He draws his conclusions not merely on a whim, but with respect to other colleagues in the field. Some of these people hold markedly skeptical and negative attitudes toward spirituality and mediumship, while others happily explore the subject and at times demonstrate an affirmative bias toward the objective reality of paranormal events.

The Italian parapsychologist Professor Ernesto Bozzano published a book in the 1920's that introduced his readership to the typical activities of consciousness at the moment of death. Bozanno gathered his research material from numerous first-hand accounts of the dying. It apparently was common for individuals to describe experiencing the presence of apparitions as they left their body. These out of body experiences and spirit encounters were accompanied by psychic bilocation[4] and at times, eerie communications between spirit mediums and the dead. Scott Rogo cites Bozanno's book as one of the earliest modern scientific texts to address the

---

[4] Bilocation: An event wherein an individual or object is located in two distinct places at the same time. Psychic bilocation typically refers to the appearance of one's ghost as a body of light, separate from the physical body.

presence of "transcendental music" during subjects' near death experiences. Bozzano apparently made careful note of this *music from the land of the dead* and has since been criticized by others in the field for his openness to the possibility that these phenomena were something other than pathological auditory hallucinations.[5]

Rogo sternly evaluates and deconstructs the propositions of one of his contemporary research fellows, Rene Sudre, based on a published text entitled *Treatise on Parapsychology* in which Sudre dismisses *"psychic music"* as having no objective correlate beyond the mind of the subject. Rogo complains about Sudre's dull, offhanded rejection of the phenomena and his unsubstantiated claim to "hordes of counter-theories" of which no actual examples are cited. Sudre seems to have completely rejected the possibility of a spirit world, whereas Bozzano seems to be convinced of its objective reality. **Rogo cites the work of Bozzano and Sudre as reflecting the most common, *polarized attitudes* in the parapsychology field. Rogo then goes on to *reject the work of both analysts*, admitting that there is yet insufficient scientific research to draw definite conclusions in either direction.**

Continuing his investigation, Rogo cycles through a number of case studies. Some are several pages in length, although for the most part only one or two sentences actually make reference to the *otherworldly music*. It is as if Rogo has taken a magnifying glass to the Near Death Experience (NDE) literature and highlighted the marginalized reports of music so as to amplify our awareness of them and identify recurrent patterns. These accounts are typically brief and a little vague. Indeed, Rogo's findings may not seem to be particularly impressive and easily dismissed. Yet it bears noting that **Rogo's steady passage through dozens of musical NDEs reveals a pattern of phenomenological constants that had previously gone unnoticed in his field**. While his inquiry sheds light on phenomenological constants, Rogo achieves this with a measure of uncertainty regarding the "objective existence" of perceived events as cited in the NDE cases.

For Rogo, the experience of **otherworldly music appears to have no fixed, external source, yet can be heard by people in normal, unaltered states of consciousness**. This observation comes not only from a study of NDE reports, but from clinically sane individuals who spontaneously hear such things - not in a dream or during a psychotic hallucination, but during mundane events of waking life. In *Casebook of Otherworldly Music*, Rogo suggests that the perception of otherworldly music is not restricted to the domain of the NDE. This thesis is supported by first hand testimony from

---

[5] Treatise on Parapsychology, Rene Sudre, Allen & Unwin, 1960

individuals near death, who commonly report hearing such sounds regardless of whether they have any medical history of psychopathology.

Not only do the dying tend to experience "celestial music", but according to numerous reports, it would appear that **friends and family gathering around the death bed often hear this music as well**, as if exhibiting a telepathic connection between themselves and the consciousness of the dying person. These telepathic connections can exert an instantaneous, non-local influence upon friends and family at a distance. Someone may realize suddenly and intuitively that their loved one has died, even if they are halfway across the world and have no reason to believe that is the case. Often times their awareness of the death is accompanied by a strange sensation of nonlocal *music*.

Descriptions of the *transcendental music* heard by its percipients share a few common qualities. For example, in nearly every case, **the sounds are described as both beautiful and strange**, tending to swell up from silence to fullness and then fading again into the distance. Both the pitch and volume are subject to change in this way. One case cited by Rogo describes a woman who would rise each morning before the sun and wait to hear its music as it came up over the horizon.[6] Generally speaking, the transcendent music is regarded as supernatural, being "felt" rather than heard with the physical ears.

Another shared quality in transcendental music shows up in Rogo's studies that would escape the layperson's observations. Rogo makes a distinction between two types of out of body experiences (OBE) in the NDE literature: the natural and the enforced. Natural out of body experiences would include normal states of ill health and exhaustion, whereas enforced OBE are triggered more suddenly and artificially, through anesthetic, falling, hypnotic trances, and suffocation. In distinguishing these two categories, **Rogo points out that the natural cases tend to hear *vocal* transcendental music while the enforced will more often hear *instrumental* transcendental music.** He hypothesizes that this relates to the immediacy of vocal music as a natural and physical expression of the body, compared to the secondary and artificial nature of instrumental music.

To fully appreciate the nature of transcendental music, Rogo insists that we should realize the commonness of ghosts and apparitions during typical OBE visionary sequences. **Often times the dying will attribute their celestial music to discarnate entities, such as the singing of angels, and in more than a few cases the light-body of these spirits are perceived**

---

[6] Fate Magazine, Nov-Dec 1951

collectively by deathbed observers. Attempting to make sense of this, Rogo posits the existence of a psychic ether and intermediate realm between mind and matter. This boundary between worlds, he says, is softened by death and its contents are revealed to the living in the form of ghostlike figures and otherworldly music. Despite his presentation of an agnostic self-image, Rogo seems to have a bias toward the actual existence of these *supraphysical* "etheric-objects". Faced with such a mountain of research data, it seems impossible to deny that people experience otherworldly music. The real question is how we explain the shared subjective experience of celestial music and spooky apparitions.

Rogo suggests that during a person's death sequence, the veil between worlds gets thin enough that the dying begin to transfer their consciousness into an "incipient apparition," an early developmental form of their *other-world* body of light. Rogo does not believe that these are purely subjective events, though he doesn't quite view them objectively either. From his perspective, the psychic field becomes a semi-permeable membrane through which the dying person's soul is meant to project itself and travel. As a result, this music and spooky imagery bleeds through into the consciousness of not only dying persons, but of those who share an intimate psychic connection with them as well. In psychological language, this amounts to an act of involuntary transference from the projective NDE/OBE to their living companions.

The greater implication of this theory seems to be that **both ghosts and transcendental music actually exist *in potential* as semi-autonomous supraphysical events.** Some people may not witness the ghosts or music during the same moment that others do, and this has created an intellectual glitch in our collective attitude toward such phenomena. Are the people reporting transcendental music simply hallucinating? If so, can we be sure that such hallucinations are merely the side effect of abnormal neurological conditions? How do we account for shared "hallucinations"? How do we explain cases where the moment of death is allied to the presence of transcendental music, which, although it cannot be assigned to a particular origin, is recognized by people on opposite sides of the planet?

The *ultimate concern*, to borrow a phrase from parapsychology, is the inevitable collapse between the objective and subjective modes of perception. Mundane sensations and psychic sensations are experienced through human consciousness as qualitatively different but essentially similar acts of *observation*. Thus it no longer serves us to speak of "hallucinations" as though they were mere projections of the mind in contrast to objectively true perceptions of a real and physical reality. To do so would be to create a sociocultural consensus that invalidates an otherwise perfectly valid, observable mode of human experience, albeit a relatively rare and subtle one. Neither does it make sense to speak of an objectively existing spiritual realm, which would be to render the subtle coarse and collapse the mystery into a flattened, iconic representation of its deeper nature.

A middle way must be intellectually formulated and innately understood, transcending the subject/object dialectic to arrive at a unified field of perception in which the observer is both the perceiver and the thing perceived. In the case of transcendental music, for example, the psychic field of a percipient has enough intrinsic and autonomous existence to be projected from the individual to a collective. Yet these collective perceptions are easily marginalized by other witnesses who claim to have experienced nothing. Very simply, one group of people will feel that something has happened and can even share some general details about the content, while another group will totally deny the existence of that event. Who has the authority to claim possession of the "objective" truth?

Several chapters in the *Casebook of Otherworldly Music* are devoted **to the presence of otherworldly music in allegedly haunted spaces.** Rogo makes reference to a variety of examples, including the chanting of phantom monks, the quiet wailing of a woman's voice in a haunted house, and faint medieval songs heard in a graveyard. From the collected body of reference texts, he offers a variety of possible theoretical interpretations. These include the telepathic theory, revised telepathic theory, psychometric theory, spirit hypothesis, and mental projection theory.

It could be that more than one class of paranormal   phenomena exists, in which case these various explanatory models may not be mutually exclusive. Having conducted a thorough investigation into these case documents, Rogo concludes that the human soul does survive death and may become a free-acting agent, a ghost, whose residence in a hypothetical *intermediary realm* grants them access to influence over physical matter, warping the psychic ether and communicating intelligently with the psychically receptive.

Could it be that this *intermediary realm* has always been accessible to human beings and was in fact the plane of experience that originally inspired philosophers to spin mythic tales about a Harmony of the Spheres?

ARE GHOSTS FLYING OUT THROUGH YOUR STEREO?

OPERATING SYSTEM

The conventional Western musical wheel is divided into twelve distinct parts, each referring to an individual note and a chain of occult correspondences. ASTROMUSIK regards these as TONE COLORS -- Not to be confused with the sound quality or timbre of an instrument.

Tone Colors will be hereafter referred to as NOTES. Dealing with the inner realm of IDEAS, these NOTES will be represented on staff paper with the understanding that they imply a whole chain of corresponding COLORS, PLANETS, ZODIACAL SIGNS, LETTERS, NUMBERS, TAROT KEYS and MORE. All the usual activities of Western Tonal Harmony are fair game. You can create auditory sigils (musical motifs that have magical power) endowed with melodic and harmonic form by which you may communicate the energy of your True Will through sound. This magical language enjoys a high degree of internal integrity. You are nevertheless free to reconfigure the attributions as you see fit.

A detailed table of correspondence will be offered in the pages that follow. Be aware that working with these Notes in your own LABORATORY may elicit spontaneous creative impulses and motivate the formulation of novel experimental procedures. Examples of what this looks like are offered in the later half of this book. Consider TONE COLOR ALCHEMY a permission slip: you have been granted the right and opportunity to take new creative risks and leap into the unknown worlds of your own sacred imagination.

OPERATOR'S MANUAL
A GLOSSARY OF MUSICAL CONNECTIONS

NOTES	COLOR	ASTROLOGICAL	TAROT
C	RED	ARIES	EMPEROR
	RED	MARS	TOWER
	RED	PLUTO	JUDGMENT
C#/Db	RED-ORANGE	TAURUS	HEIROPHANT
D	ORANGE	GEMINI	LOVERS
	ORANGE	SOL	THE SUN
D#/Eb	ORANGE-YELLOW	CANCER	CHARIOT
E	YELLOW	URANUS	FOOL
	YELLOW	MERCURY	MAGICIAN
	YELLOW	LEO	STRENGTH
F	YELLOW-GREEN	VIRGO	HERMIT
F#/Gb	GREEN	VENUS	EMPRESS
	GREEN	LIBRA	JUSTICE
G	GREEN-BLUE	SCORPIO	DEATH
G#/Ab	BLUE	LUNA	PRIESTESS
	BLUE	NEPTUNE	HANGED MAN
	BLUE	SAGGITARIUS	TEMPERANCE
A	BLUE-VIOLET	CAPRICORN	DEVIL
	BLUE-VIOLET	SATURN	WORLD
A#/Bb	VIOLET	JUPITER	FORTUNE
	VIOLET	AQUARIUS	STAR
B	VIOLET-RED	PISCES	THE MOON

Author's Note: You can contact the *Builders of the Adytum* for deeper initiation into the intended use of these tone-color correspondences. Paul Foster Case was the first to publicly correlate the Golden Dawn's King Scale system to musical notes and he did so with clear intentions for angelic invocation and soul development. I prefer to explore its unorthodox application to en-spirited music composition and divination.

"There are no rules anywhere." – Malaclypse the Younger, *Principia Discordia*

THE TWENTY-TWO TRUMPS OF TAROT

1) א: FOOL - Spontaneous Impulse Towards Individuation

2) ב: MAGICIAN - Communication and Manifestation Skills

3) ג: HIGH PRIESTESS – Memory, Feelings, Instinct, Intuition

4) ד: EMPRESS - Magnetic Love, Sex, Intelligence of Nature

5) ה: EMPEROR - Confidence, Ambition, Trust, Sovereignty

6) ו: HIEROPHANT – Convention, Tradition, Rules, Religion

7) ז: LOVERS - Romantic Love, Sex, Marriage, Partnership

8) ח: CHARIOT - Battles, Advancing Forward, Protective Shells

9) ט: STRENGTH - Courage and Triumph, Winning, Success

10) י: HERMIT - Solitude & Introspection, Guardian of Mysteries

20) כ: WHEEL OF FORTUNE - Time Cycles, Luck, Fortune

30) ל: JUSTICE - Balanced Observations and the Law of Karma

40) מ: HANGED MAN - Self-Sacrifice and the Art of Surrender

50) נ: DEATH - Intensity, Confrontation, Completion

60) ס: TEMPERANCE - Peaceful and Harmonizing Influence

70) ע: DEVIL - Temptation, Bondage, Greed, Lust, Slavery

80) פ: TOWER - Chaos, Destruction, the Mood of Apocalypse

90) צ: STAR - Hope, Faith, Solution-Orientation, Optimism

100) ק: MOON - Illusions, Deception, Mirage, the Dreaming

200) ר: SUN - Happiness, Good Health, Prosperity, Radiance

300) ש: JUDGMENT - Revelations and New Beginnings; Rebirth

400) ת: WORLD - Arrival, Reward, The Wish-Come-True

THE ZODIAC AND PLANETS

The Role of Astrology in Civilization and Human Psychology

A study of ancient human civilization and mythology reveals that our ancestors experienced life on Earth as a dense reflection of subtle, higher-dimensional activities. Astrologers examined macrocosmic cycles in the sky in relation to life on this planet in order to better know God and live with a deeper sense of purpose. Earth-based cultures revered life as an ongoing series of magical acts that expressed the will of our planetary World Soul, while Monotheists proposed that our planetary soul was merely a tendril of God's will. The most spiritually advanced traditions honored both of these perspectives, and ultimately, regardless of a culture's religious beliefs, everyone studied astronomy.

The Chinese, Greek, Egyptian, and Mesoamerican intelligentsia established methods to predict and dictate world events based on these celestial patterns. Astronomers played Connect The Dots with the distances between stars and planets, taking careful measurements and recording them over long periods of time. Knowledge gained from astronomy was then applied to terrestrial dynamics like civic and agricultural engineering.

The main difference between astronomy and astrology is the application of human imagination to astral mathematics. Astrological myths, though often remarkably similar to one another, vary significantly from culture to culture and therefore may be regarded as non-universal projective phenomena of the mind. The physical constellation of Sagittarius, for example, had nothing to do with the Western interpretation of it as *the archer* or the psychological impulse to *explore* until someone portrayed it that way. The luminosity of astrological motifs comes from its source deep within the structures of the human psyche, shaped over many eons by the collective human experience and our propensity for storytelling.

The stars do not have the meaning individuals attribute to them until, through repetition, a culture formulates some concrete ideas about their signification. Any time that people in a given culture begin to tell themselves a new story, they reinterpret and recreate an entirely different universe of meaning for the cosmos. Thus, all observable phenomena, especially something as distant as the stars and planets, amount to a kind of inkblot, drawing forth projections from the open-ended depths of inner space.

Mythology presents us with an opportunity to organize mental perception in a way that opens us up to multiple roads of self-realization. Our natal chart can be interpreted in a way that gently steers us through life upon a network of symbols and metaphysical essences. The same goes for the intervals of musical harmony, whose qualitative difference we can feel intuitively, and which today holds a wealth of personal and collective meanings, offering up a rich legacy of culturally evolved symbols that were absent during the earliest human experiments.

Thus in both the experience, analysis, and composition of music, as well as the interpretation of astrological data, it is essential that we keep an open mind and search for ways in which sound can invigorate our quest to know ourselves. Listening to music sheds light on our blind spots and reveals to us our unconscious, unexamined and self-limiting assumptions. So too does the game of astrology. These techniques of inquiry permit us to question and release concepts that no longer serve us, replacing them with liberating and open-ended notions about ourselves. In so doing we naturally embrace, evolve, and craft new stories about the Self that resonate authentically with our lives and guide us toward our highest purpose.

Antithetical to the spirit of creative interpretation is fatalism. Astrological *determinism* suggests that a person's sun, moon and rising signs spell out a predetermined *fate*. Is the cosmos really so rigid? Myths and dreams need not prescribe someone's life with a predestined and inevitable outcome. In fact, to do so might artificially restrict and undermine the organic life of astrological archetypes. Star signs represent a rich and fluidic realm of many-to-many mappings, which like music, take on different meanings from one person to the next.

Three dimensions of symbolic language interact at different levels to produce the various meanings derived from Western astrology. At the center of this semiotic trinity is planet Earth, and in relationship to it the worlds of *planets, signs, and houses*. Each of these symbol sets represents a central aspect of the human being. When arranged in the unique combinations of our natal chart, or in the various transits of our day-to-day experience, the planets/signs/houses paint a picture of co-informative influences whose effects can then be observed and harnessed by the astrologer. What follows is a brief overview of how these categories are defined, so as to better understand their relationship to the art of speculative music.

Generally speaking, the zodiacal **signs** represent psychological templates of identity. They differ from one another subtly but unequivocally. Each category represents a conglomerate of mental attitudes, beliefs and ways of perception symbolized by the essence of their mythic representatives. Aries, for example, is represented by the image of a ram, charging forward like a warrior and pioneer. As the first sign in the series of twelve, it relates to the early impulses of springtime and the dawning of new life. Put succinctly, it relates to one's identification with courage and bravery.

The **planets** symbolize the various psychological functions that inform how we engage with our environment, including but not limited to categories of intellect, emotions, intuition, and so forth. Each planet can potentially manifest itself in either a healthy or dysfunctional way, depending on how we dream it. The planets express themselves during a given moment through the medium of their resident sign. Aries could be occupied by its ruling planet Mars, the planetary representative of assertiveness, to manifest as an aggressive display of power. In contrast, the loving nature of Venus could show up in the sign of Aries as a stabilizing influence, tempering the explosive power of the ram with the wisdom of the mothering principle.

Only when we apply the planets and their resident signs to the **houses** do we arrive at a complete picture of cosmic influences upon our life. Each house indicates a different socio-cultural sphere through which the planet-sign pairs operate, rendering their energized identities visible through various theatres of activity, such as marriage, career or travel. When the loving nature of Venus is conditioned by identification with the courageous and impulsive Aries, it may extend its influence into the third house, the house of communication, as a bold and compassionate willingness to talk through social disagreements. Mars-in-Aries on the other hand may struggle with third-house communication skills, tending to push their perspective aggressively at the expense of the other.

The only major planet missing from conventional Western astrology is Earth. As a geocentric model of the universe, astrology describes events on Earth through the lens of the Other (i.e. The Heavens). What then is the role of our planet in the cosmic drama? I personally believe that Earth is a conscious being. Much more than a biological host to be exploited at will by the human race, our planet is actively dreaming up all terrestrial life forms to perceive and respond to one other in a way that fulfills her own needs and impulses. Every living plant and creature is a character whose performance represents in embodied, physical form an interaction that the *Mother* wishes to have with herself.

Whether you subscribe to the mother-earth script or not, the following can be stated with certainty; The language of astrology maps the psychological life of humanity in a way that is non-prescriptive, technical and scientific in its astronomical observations while artful and poetic in its mythic attributions. Our birth chart and its transits feature a whole collection of planet-sign-house combos that can be studied and interpreted symbolically to bring clarity our life. Let's have a look at the myths of planets and signs in Western astrology to further clarify this point.

Focal Point of Personality

Sol

Tone-Color: D Natural - Orange

Tarot Card: The Sun

Mode of Intelligence: Ego (Self-Image)

Musical Icon: "Was a Sunny Day" – Paul Simon

Keywords

Source of Light and Life-Force Energy

Gravitational Center of the Soul

Orientation in Life

Unifying Mode of Consciousness

Vitality of Spirit

Perseverance and Stamina

Decision Making Faculties

Will to Action

Radiance and Confidence

Personal Power

Health

Emotional Response to Life

Luna

☽

Tone-Color:	G-Sharp (A-Flat) / Blue
Tarot Card:	The High Priestess
Mode of Intelligence:	Receptivity and Sensitivity
Musical Icon:	"Moonlight Sonata" – Beethoven

Keywords

Cycles of Change

Emotional Intelligence

Moods and Feelings

Subjective Instincts and Impulses

Unmitigated Expressions of Psychic Energy

Irrational Reactions to our Experience

Rise and fall of the Ocean Tide

Rhythms of Nature

Free flow of Ideas and Imagination

Desires and Attachments

Communication Skills

Mercury

Tone-Color:	E Natural / Yellow
Tarot Card:	The Magician
Mode of Intelligence:	Information Exchange
Musical Icon:	"Flight of the Bumblebee" – Rimsky-Korsakov

Keywords

Communication and the Use of Language

Abstract Forms and Images

Patterns of Thought (*Thoth*)

Mental Activity

Information Processing

Ability to Prove Anything

Shape-Shifting Intellect

Thinking for Yourself

Service to Self

Transformations within the Imagination

Love and Heart

Venus

♀

Tone-Color:	F Sharp (G Flat)/ Green
Tarot Card:	The Empress
Mode of Intelligence:	Intimate Relationships
Musical Icon:	"There is No Greater Love" – Four Freshman

Keywords

Impulse to Nurture and Nourish

Romance and Fulfillment of Desires

Balance in Personal Relationships

Beauty Elegance and Equilibrium

Aesthetic and Artistic Preferences

Longing for Pleasurable Sensations

Animal Magnetism

Seductive Powers of Sexuality

Luxury and Creature Comforts

Preoccupations with How We Appear to the World

Taking Direct Action

Mars

♂

Tone-Color:	C Natural - Red
Tarot Card:	The Tower
Mode of Intelligence:	Courage and Will
Musical Icon:	"The Imperial March" – Star Wars (Williams)

Keywords

War Combat and Martial Arts

Fearlessness and Consistency

Domination and Assertiveness

Rage Anger and Cruelty

Aggressive Imposition of Will Power

Reacting Impulsively to Irritation

Pointless Acts of Violence Rape and Abuse

Annihilation of Whatever Stands in Our Way

Will to Survive at All Costs

Sex Drive and Blood Flow

Expanding with Optimism

Jupiter

♃

Tone-Color:	B-Flat (A-Sharp) - Violet
Tarot Card:	The Wheel of Fortune
Mode of Intelligence:	Faith and Confidence
Musical Icon:	"New York, New York" – Frank Sinatra

Keywords

Joy Laughter and Self-Confidence

Feeling Inspired by New Possibilities

Remaining Open while Holding True to our Beliefs

Luck and Good Fortune

Commitment rooted in Faith.

Feeling Larger than Life

Exaggeration and Inflation

Generosity rooted in the Dominion over Others

Making Demands based on Expectations

The Benevolent Dictator

Self-Discipline

Saturn

♄

Tone-Color:	A Natural – Blue-Violet
Tarot Card:	The World
Mode of Intelligence:	Limitations and Boundaries
Musical Icon:	"O Fortuna" – Carl Orff

Keywords

Clocks and Strict Measurements

Stress Difficulties and Hard Work

Taking Responsibility for our Actions

Growing up and Acting like an Adult

Tangible Accomplishments

The Devouring Father/ Satan (Saturn)

Professional Commitments and Contracts

Slowness Materialism and Density

Depression and Pessimism

Earning a Living

Individuality

Uranus

⛢

Tone-Color:	E Natural – Yellow
Tarot Card:	The Fool
Mode of Intelligence:	Power to Question Authority
Musical Icon:	"Iorxhscimtor" – Orthrelm

Keywords

Refusal to Conform to the Demands of Society

Unpredictable High Weirdness Shock!!

Reprogramming Internal Tendencies of Perception

Developing Self-Awareness

The Will to Be Free

Defending What We Know to Be True

Conscious and Informed Decision-Making.

Sovereignty and Autonomy despite Restrictions

Liberation from Artificial Boundaries

Transgressive Activities

Dreaming

Neptune

♆

Tone-Color:	G-Sharp (A-Flat) – Blue
Tarot Card:	The Hanged Man
Mode of Intelligence:	Night and Day Dreams
Musical Icon:	"Choirs of the Eye" – Kayo Dot

Keywords

Strange Visions and Miracles

Merging with Transpersonal Psychic Influences

Dismantling the Ego

Dreamtime and Disembodied States

Viewing Oneself from Outside Oneself

Blank Slates and Hypnotic States

Emptiness of Mind

Compassion through Boundary Dissolution

Prayer Contemplation and Meditation

Extrasensory Perception and Psychic Lucidity

Transmutation

Pluto

⯓

Tone-Color:	C Natural – Red
Tarot Card:	Judgment
Mode of Intelligence:	Psychic Death and Rebirth
Musical Icon:	"Astronome Act III" – Mike Patton and Zorn

Keywords

Our Deepest Fear

Our Greatest Treasure

Transformation by way of Psychic Annihilation

Being a Stranger to Oneself

Hell Realms and the Immense Power of Death

Unapologetically Channeling the Daemonic

Intelligence that transcends Morality and Dogma

Arrogant and Dictatorial Vanity

Possession by Transpersonal Forces

Maximum Intensity

The First Sign

<u>ARIES (The Ram)</u>

<u>♈</u>

Tone-Color:	C Natural / Red
Elemental Mode:	Cardinal Fire
Tarot Card:	The Emperor
Embodiment:	King – Soldier – Explorer
Musical Icon:	"Rite of Spring" – Igor Stravinsky

<u>Keywords</u>

Life Force Energy

Breaking Through Previous Limitations

The Will to Be in the World

Courage to Confront and Overcome Obstacles

Selfishness With Heart

The Fearless Warrior

Positive Stress and the Pressure Cooker

Motivation to Pursue and Accomplish Goals

Excitement and the Evolutionary Impulse

The Second Sign

TAURUS (The Bull)

♉

Tone-Color:	C Sharp (D Flat) / Red-Orange
Elemental Mode:	Fixed Earth
Tarot Card:	The Hierophant
Embodiment:	Meditating Yogi – Priest – Sage
Musical Icon:	"Besame Mucho" – Joao Gilberto

Keywords

Strength and Sensuality

Winning the War to Arrive at Peace

Overcoming the Desire to be Perceived as Fearless

Enjoying Rest and Relaxation

Sitting Quietly and Listening Carefully

Safety from the Extremes of Passion and Desire

Disengaging the Drama

Hanging out at Home

Feeling Grounded and Stable

The Third Sign

GEMINI (The Twins)

Ⅱ

Tone-Color:	D Natural / Orange
Elemental Mode:	Mutable Air
Tarot Card:	The Lovers
Embodiment:	Partners – Collaborators – Soul Mates
Musical Icon:	"Dueling Banjos" – Arthur Smith

Keywords

Communication: Speaking and Listening

Constant Movement and Equivalent Exchange

Sacred Reciprocity and Mutual Support

Intuitively Unraveling the Mystery

Making Sense of it All

Asking Questions and Giving Answers

Inviting the Unknown

Open-Minded Acceptance of Chaos

Sifting Through Information

The Fourth Sign

CANCER (The Crab)

Tone-Color:	D Sharp (E Flat) / Orange-Yellow
Elemental Mode:	Cardinal Water
Tarot Card:	The Chariot
Embodiment:	Mother – Nurturer – Caretaker
Musical Icon:	"The Nymphs" – John Zorn

Keywords

Introversion

Identity Armor

Protecting Our Vulnerability

Guarding against the World

Defense and Protection

Anonymity and Shyness

Deep Relationship to the Inner Sense of Self

The Inner Compass of Feeling and Intuition

Desire to Help Support and Heal Others

The Fifth Sign

LEO (The Lion)

♌

Tone-Color:	E Natural / Yellow
Elemental Mode:	Fixed Fire
Tarot Card:	Strength
Embodiment:	Rock Star – Royalty – Performance Artist
Musical Icon:	"Sun King" – The Beatles

Keywords

Reveling in Self-Image and Ego

Expressing the Inner Life out in the World

Embodying aspects of the Great Mystery

Improvised and Spontaneous Performances

Displays of Confidence Pride and Power

Playful and Childlike Disposition

Happiness and Generosity of Spirit

Grandiosity, Arrogance, and Self-Importance

Charisma is a Charm

The Sixth Sign

Virgo (The Virgin)

♍

Tone-Color:	F Natural / Yellow-Green
Elemental Mode:	Mutable Earth
Tarot Card:	The Hermit
Embodiment:	Saint – Martyr – Servant
Musical Icon:	"A Rose for Emily" – The Zombies

Keywords

Perfectionism and the Pursuit of an Ideal

The Analytical Mind that Dissects Everything

The Control Freak and the Inner Critic

Service to the Other as an Ego-Strategy

Idealistic Values and Desire to be Pure

The Hardworking Busybody

Professionalism and Attention to Detail

Self-Sacrifice and the potential for Self-Destruction

Calculated Generosity

The Seventh Sign

Libra (The Scales)

Ω

Tone-Color:	F Sharp (G Flat) / Green
Elemental Mode:	Cardinal Air
Tarot Card:	Justice
Embodiment:	Judge – Artisan – Philosopher
Musical Icon:	"Court of the Crimson King" – King Crimson

Keywords

Balance of Opposites

Feeling Okay with Paradox and Contradictions

Weighing the Options and Creating Harmony

Coming to Terms with Chaos and Disorder

Compassion, Tolerance and Mercy

Judgment of Self and Others

Diplomacy and Compromises

Creating Mutual Understanding

Ambiguity and the Plague of Indecision

The Eighth Sign

Scorpio (The Eagle)

♏

Tone-Color:	G Natural / Green-Blue
Elemental Mode:	Fixed Water
Tarot Card:	Death
Embodiment:	Outlaw – Mercenary – Sorcerer
Musical Icon:	"Electric Funeral" – Black Sabbath

Keywords

Awareness of Death

Intensity of the Present Moment

Willingness to Feel Any and All Emotions

Unrepressed Sexuality and Emotional Intimacy

Overwhelming and Disturbing Realizations

Dissolution as a path to deeper Self-Awareness

Introspective Moodiness

Clairvoyance and Unflinching Awareness

Precision and the Eagle Eye

The Ninth Sign

Sagittarius (The Archer)

Tone-Color:	G Sharp (A Flat) / Blue
Elemental Mode:	Mutable Fire
Tarot Card:	Temperance
Embodiment:	Traveler – Philosopher – Explorer
Musical Icon:	"Heart of the Sunrise" - Yes

Keywords

Exploring New Horizons

Setting Personal Goals

Accumulating New Experiences

Discovering and Enjoying Foreign Worldviews

Searching for the Meaning of Life

Sublimely Open-Ended Processes

Pushing the Boundaries

Valuing Experience over Concepts

Sense of Humor Optimism and Curiosity

The Tenth Sign

Capricorn (The Goat-Fish)

♑

Tone-Color:	A Natural / Blue-Violet
Elemental Mode:	Cardinal Earth
Tarot Card:	The Devil
Embodiment:	Boss – Master – Tyrant
Musical Icon:	"Hall of the Mountain King" – Grieg

Keywords

Hunger for Power

Taking Advantage of Others for Personal Gain

Gratification of Desires

Opportunistic Organisms

Integration of the Shadow

Unapologetic and Aggressive Self-Interest

Solitude and Strength

Self-Respect and Discipline

Creating and Utilizing Boundaries

The Eleventh Sign

Aquarius (The Water-Bearer)

♒

Tone-Color:	A-Sharp (B-Flat) / Violet
Elemental Mode:	Fixed Air
Tarot Card:	The Star
Embodiment:	Gifted – Genius – Non-Conformist
Musical Icon:	"Maggie's Farm" – Bob Dylan

Keywords

Individuation

Refusal to Surrender to Social Norms

Renegade and Iconoclast

Defining New Value Systems

Unwillingness to Compromise

Seeing Through Illusion

Capacity to Know Something with Certainty

Alienation and Marginalized Existence

Viva la Resistance!

The Twelfth Sign

Pisces (Pair of Fish)

♓

Tone-Color:	B Natural / Violet-Red
Elemental Mode:	Mutable Water
Tarot Card:	The Moon
Embodiment:	Dreamer – Artist – Shaman
Musical Icon:	"Clair De Lune" – Claude Debussy

Keywords

Daydreaming

Contemplating the Mysteries of Existence

Taking Refuge in the act of Perception itself

Mysticism without Dogma

Free-Associative Power of the Imagination

Poetry Music and Sacred Geometry

Sensitivity to the Feelings of Others

Escapism Addiction and Fantasies

Dissociative Relationship to the Ego Structure

Recapitulation of the

TROPICAL ZODIAC SIGNS

♈ **ARIES** : Courage to Face and Overcome Obstacles

♉ **TAURUS** : Abiding Peacefully in a State of Rest

♊ **GEMINI** : Reciprocal Communication with Others

♋ **CANCER** : Defense/Protection and Introversion

♌ **LEO** : Proud and Confident Displays of the Ego

♍ **VIRGO** : Organization and Devoted Service Work

♎ **LIBRA** : Measuring and Harmonizing Opposites

♏ **SCORPIO** : Intense Emotions and Instincts

♐ **SAGITTARIUS** : Happily Exploring the Unknown

♑ **CAPRICORN** : Authority Informed by Self-Interest

♒ **AQUARIUS** : Rebellion against Authority Figures

♓ **PISCES** : Consciousness and the Divine Witness

Recapitulation of the

PLANETARY AGENTS

☉ **SOL :** Center of the Personal Identity (Ego)

☽ **LUNA :** Emotional Reactions to Experience

☿ **MERCURY :** Language and Communication

♀ **VENUS :** Pleasure & Intimate Relationships

♂ **MARS :** Directional Focus and Willpower

♃ **JUPITER :** Optimism about Commitments

♄ **SATURN :** Severity & Strict Commitments

♅ **URANUS :** Eccentricity and Individualism

♆ **NEPTUNE :** Dreamtime and Dissociation

♇ **PLUTO :** Embodiment of Transpersonal Will

Illuminating the Influence of

PLANETS IN THE ZODIACAL SIGNS

☉ ☽ ☿ ♀ ♂ ♃ ♄ ♅ ♆ ♀

Astrologers tend to think about the relationship between Planets and Signs in their practical application to *Natal and Transit Charts*. Another term for the Natal Chart is the Birth Chart. Everything that happens after the moment of our birth is considered a Transit, or snapshot of planetary bodies in the sky at that moment. The planets can be framed as psychic impulses coming from within, expressed through the filter of whatever zodiacal sign they currently inhabit. A third factor in these charts, called the Houses, determines which areas of our personal life these Planetary-Zodiacal influences are tangibly manifesting in. An accurate interpretation of astrological charts requires that the planets, signs, and houses be co-contemplated as a unified field, superimposed onto the life of the person in question to derive meaningful information about their inner life. Meditating upon these astro-mandalas can draw unconscious projections up and out of us, revealing the contents of our mind and exposing emotional states that we may not have been aware of, while simultaneously confirming and affirming what we already knew.

Determining the meaning of a planetary-zodiacal configuration requires skillfulness and creativity on the part of the interpreter. As symbols of deep psychodynamic processes, they cannot be easily reduced to simple aphorisms and catchphrases. The benefit of working with the Zodiacal Houses is that it narrows our attention to specific areas of our experience, such as our career, romantic, or family life taking the abstract psychological principles of planet-sign combinations and applying it to every day experiences. The following pages will explore the basics of this technique so that you can work with your own natal and transit charts. Learning this art form will grant deeper psychological meaning to the musical divination experiments of **Tone Color Alchemy**.

♈ ♉ ♊ ♋ ♌ ♍ ♎ ♏ ♐ ♑ ♒ ♓

Real Life Manifestation

THE TWELVE HOUSES

FIRST HOUSE :   *Personality and Identity*

SECOND HOUSE :   *Finances and Possessions*

THIRD HOUSE :   *Communication*

FOURTH HOUSE :   *Home and Solitude*

FIFTH HOUSE :   *Children and Playfulness*

SIXTH HOUSE :   *Devotion & Responsibility*

SEVENTH HOUSE :   *Marriage and Intimacy*

EIGHTH HOUSE :   *Sexuality and Death*

NINTH HOUSE :   *Travel and Exploration*

TENTH HOUSE :   *Career and Reputation*

ELEVENTH HOUSE : *Community Affiliations*

TWELFTH HOUSE :   *Uncertainty and Problems*

- -

Houses inform our understanding of **how** the archetypal energies symbolized by Planet-Sign combos will find expression in our lives. You may have noticed that the meaning of each House is closely related to the corresponding positions of the Signs. The difference between them is that signs give shape and form to our encounter with the planetary forces, whereas the twelve Houses let us know where in our life each one of these unique planet-sign combos will be taking effect.

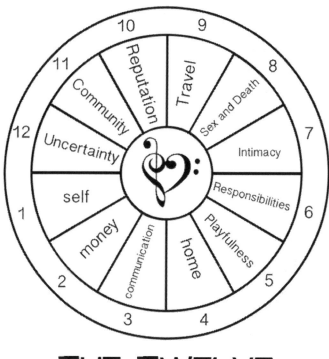

THE TWELVE HOUSES

This map represents a panoramic view of the sky from Earth. Houses One through Six are positioned beneath the horizon and are therefore not visible. Houses Seven through Twelve are positioned above the horizon and are visible. You can use this key to make sense of your birth chart. The planet-sign combinations are explicitly marked with the appropriate astrological symbols whereas the houses are delineated only by segments of the circle. Keep in mind that, in contrast to the twelve signs, the twelve houses are not divided up equally. Please turn the page for an applied example.

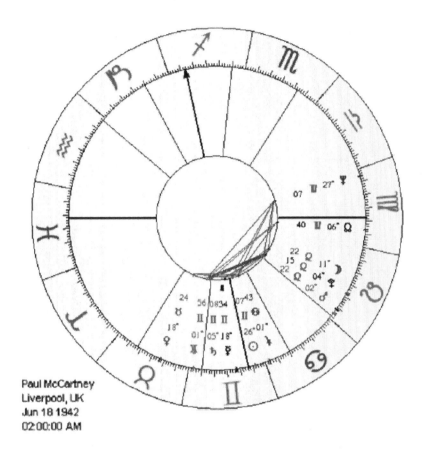

Paul McCartney
Liverpool, UK
Jun 18 1942
02:00:00 AM

Paul McCartney

Born in Liverpool, England on June 18, 1942 at 2:00 AM

Let's take a look at Paul McCartney's Natal Chart for an example of how this works. As you can see, the twelve signs of the zodiac are positioned at the outer perimeter of the circle in 30-degree segments, equidistant from each other. The planets are located in the middle segment of the circle, leaving a tick-mark on the segmented zodiac sign with a number indicating where on the 0-30 degree range they fall. For example, the Sun ☉ is positioned 26 degrees in Gemini ♊. The Twelve Houses are non-equidistant segments in the same middle segment of the circle where the planets are located. They are represented by the radial lines. For example, the first house included half of Pisces, all of Aries, and a third of Taurus. Paul's Sun-in-Gemini is located in the Third House.

Applying a Creative Interpretation to

PAUL McCARTNEY'S NATAL CHART

Ascendant in ♓ : Self-Image defined by Creativity & Imagination

☉ *in* ♊ : Communication with others plays critical role in Self-Image

☽ *in* ♌ : Tendency to feel playful and proud of one's own Self-Image

☿ *in* ♊ : Smooth-talker that effortlessly navigates social situations

♀ *in* ♉ : Peaceful Lover who appreciates pleasurable sensations

♂ *in* ♌ : Playful-on-Purpose with a magnetic personality

♃ *in* ♋ : Feels confident and optimistic when safe from the World

♄ *in* ♊ : Can use logic and reason to adapt to interpersonal situations

♅ *in* ♊ : Feels most himself when sharing in meaningful exchanges

♆ *in* ♍ : Dreams and Creativity are organized and put to work

♇ *in* ♌ : Transformative Spiritual experiences come through Fame

- -

Paul McCartney was born with four planets in Gemini and three in Leo. An astrologer would seek to understand his personality based on these clues. Paul's Sun, Mercury, and Saturn are in *third house* Gemini and the third house corresponds to communication. To have Mercury in Third House Gemini suggests strong adaptive communication skills, a major asset for any famous public figure. His Moon, Mars, and Pluto in *sixth house* Leo grant him the emotional confidence and will power to face his worldly responsibilities with joy and playfulness. His pragmatic and intimate embodiment of the **Artist** shows up in his Pisces ascendant and Neptune in *Seventh House* Virgo.

Note: *There have been disagreements about whether Paul was born at 2 a.m. or 2 p.m.*

ASTROMUSIK THEORY

Alchemical Archetypes in Western Tonal Harmony

Let's start with the basics. When a musical string is divided in half (1:2) its pitch doubles and expresses the interval of an octave, whose acoustic sound frequency is double that of the original note. This inverse relationship between string length and pitch value has to do with basic physics of vibrating bodies. If for example an open string were tuned to the musical note C at 256hz and was pressed against a fret board at precisely half the distance between the bridge and nut of the instrument, its frequency would double to C'512hz as the higher octave of the initial tone. The length of piano strings work in a similar way, where the doubling and halving of string lengths generates the higher and lower octaves respectively.

This 1:2 octave ratio is a first law in musical harmony, essential to defining the sonic parameters within which its musical scales are delineated. Like the completion of a twelve-month cycle over the course of one year, western music has divided the octave into twelve notes so that the thirteenth note reiterates the first. Unlike the cyclical passage of months during a year, however, the subdivided musical octave expresses a passage through sound frequencies that *can* but does not *have to* proceed in a stepwise, linear fashion. Whereas the calendric model forbids that we would pass from January to September to March over the course of a few days, this is precisely what one does with the musical scale when creating a melody, and without any temporal constraints whatsoever. Thus while the octave interval resembles the completion of a time-cycle, be it the twelve months of a year or twelve hours on a clock face, the trans-linearity of musical order defies the laws of sequential time as we would typically understand it and in this way is distinct from our Western clock and calendar systems.

The ascending and descending intervals of the octave will always produce the same note, albeit at different pitches, making the 1:2 ratio an incomplete source for the derivation of musical harmony. We need the next whole number ratio in the ordinal whole-number sequence, namely the interval of 2:3, to produce a musical note that differs from the fundamental tone. When the length of a string is modified at the 2:3 ratio it produces an interval known in the Western canon as a *perfect fifth*.

Our first example, the ratio of 1:2, produced the same *note* at different pitch values, but when we apply the perfect fifth interval to a note, it produces a tone that differs from the first in both pitch *and* note value. This disidentification and departure from the original musical note produced an interesting puzzle for the early philosophers to contemplate. Was there an underlying, mathematical unity by which this simple, whole number number ratio would eventually fold back in upon itself and express the original note at a higher octave?

Pythagoras demonstrated that the interval ratio of 3:2 could indeed be expressed as a musical relationship between two notes, stacked vertically a total of twelve times to arrive back at the original note. The resulting tone would arrive approximately seven octaves above the initial, fundamental pitch[7]. A linear passage through all twelve notes was given the name "*Cycle of Fifths*". When rearranged so that the twelve notes fell within a single octave, this cycle of fifths was transformed into a "*Chromatic Scale*".

88 keys on the piano

88 days in Mercurial Orbit

The orbital cycle of Mercury is equal to approximately 88 days on Earth.[8] Just as the twelve months of an Earth year relate loosely to the twelve notes of a chromatic scale, the 88-note keyboard could be interpreted symbolically as an icon of the Mercurial year, each note representing one day of the planet's journey around the sun. In Greek and Roman mythology,

---

[7] This slight discrepancy is called the "Pythagorean comma".
[8] Mercury's orbit is 87.969 days long.

Hermes-Mercury accomplished his magical operations with a *caduceus*, or *winged staff*. Coincidentally, the horizontal ledger lines of piano sheet music are called the *grand staff*. They were originally called by the Latin name *pentagramma*, meaning five-lettered, invoking the symbol of the pentagram and contributing further to the staff's magical significance.

Mercury's caduceus staff features two serpents coiling upward around the central pillar in opposite directions. The twin snakes resemble two figure eights stacked upon each other, as if hinting at the number eighty-eight. The expression *"musical scales"* connects to the idea of *serpent scales* as recurring patterns by which one can effectively take measurements of length. If rotated horizontally, Mercury's staff transforms into a musical staff, the twin snakes resembling ascending and descending musical scales.

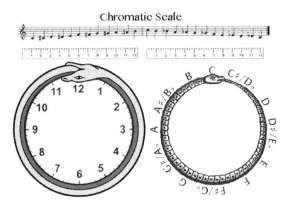

The piano's passage of scalar ascent through multiple octaves summons the image of the *ouroboros*, a higher-dimensional self-regenerating serpent that swallows its own tail. The first and final notes of a scale are separated by the interval of an octave, so that the final note mirrors the first note and replicates the scale at the next octave. In its self-similarity, the octave interval resembles the conjoined head and tail of the ouroboros serpent.

Through free associative symbolic play we can derive a wealth of meaningful clues to the alchemical and astrological philosophical influences upon the foundations of Western tonal harmony. A symbol of wholeness and completion, that magical *ring* embodied by the ouroboros etymologically suggests a musical tone, as in the ringing of a bell. As Mercury travels upon the elliptical ring of its orbit, Pythagoras would have said that it was contributing to the harmony of the spheres, and in this way the "ringing" of Mercury has to do with its unique planetary vibration as it spins through space.

Composed of twelve equally spaced half-tones, the chromatic scale is like a *key-ring*, in the sense that all twelve major and minor keys are attached to and derived from it. Symbolically, the purpose of a key is to unlock something. The availability of all twelve tones in a chromatic scale could be likened to the idea of a *skeleton key*, capable of unlocking every musical door. From the chromatic scale we derived the twelve major and minor keys, each featuring a collection of seven notes. When the same seven musical notes are predominant in a piece of music, a *home key* is established. This tonal center becomes a point of departure and return around which a piece of music defines itself.

The hermetic axiom *'As Above, So Below'* hints at this first-note and eighth-note similarity of the octave interval. Completion of a seven-note scale is achieved by expressing this reiterative eighth note. When divided in half, the eight tones form *two identical tetrachords*[9] separated by a whole step interval. Out of this hemispheric balance we can derive another play-on-words, the symbolic "balancing scales" of Libra.

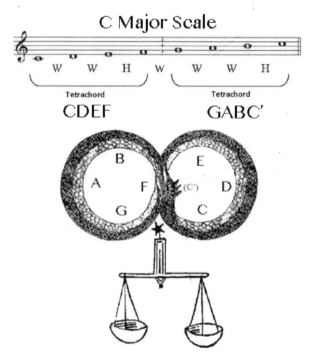

Serpentine Scales of Balanced Musical Intervals

---

[9] Tetrachord: A four-note musical scale that doubles to form a diatonic scale.

Unlike equidistant markings on a ruler, the intervals of a seven-tone *diatonic* scale are not spaced uniformly. They begin on the root note and move stepwise through a combination of whole and half tones. A major scale sequence is composed of Root-Whole-Whole-Half-Whole-Whole-Whole-Half intervals. Depending on the chosen root note, or starting point, diatonic scales can express up to 12 distinct musical keys, each scale unlocking a different tonal center.

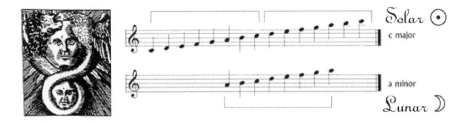

Solar ☉
c major

a minor
Lunar ☽

Every *major* scale has a *relative minor* scale made up of precisely the same notes. The difference between them is define by their starting point, or what theorists call the *root note* of their musical scale. When a song is written in a major key, its root is located in the first scale degree. The relative minor scale begins on the sixth scale degree relative to this major scale. For example, the root note of A minor (**ABCDEFGA**) is the sixth note of the C major scale (**CFEFGABC**). Conventional music theory offers no mythic explanation for the reason behind the orientation of the minor mode on the sixth scale degree. It is up to the speculative musicologist to make up his or her own mind about such matters.

From the awareness of musical scales, we can begin viewing different forms in terms of the relative similarities and differences between them. Each of the twelve major keys is linked up to a relative minor key. Archetypally, the Major key tends to express "solar" energy, while the minor key expresses "lunar" energy. The qualities of light-vibration emanating from these two astral bodies have been subtly encoded into our perception of sound-vibration through the conventions of Western harmony. Over the past three centuries, we have developed a lexicon of musical meaning that makes frequent use of the major and minor keys as extratextual musical principles. Like the yin-yang symbol of Taoist philosophy, the solar and lunar lights of Western philosophy are viewed as interdependent opposites.

Music extends from the creative unity-point of sonic singularity into a harmonic multiplicity of tones, each one expressing an immensely powerful and individuated essence. Each musical note behaves like a node in an interdependent webbing and wedding of intervals.

Human beings tend to map and relate to the world with lattices of polarity. Over millennia, our nervous system has become wired for perceiving reality through relativity and duality, drawing upon the four directions as a tool for navigating the space-time matrix of every day life. One of our roles as sentient beings on this planet is to hold the ongoing tension of opposites in our awareness, developing a psychic muscle that bridges polarities to arrive at unity. The polarity of sun and moon share a common essence as astral bodies of Light. Sound-vibration teaches us about the principles of spiritual light through analogous patterns of musical structure and resonance.

The German musical term *tongeschlect* translates as *tone gender*, suggesting that the interval relationships between tones can be viewed through the psychosexual dynamics of human relationship. Tone *genders* cannot be identified independent from interval relationships due to the androgynous and self-referential nature of individual notes. Each tone is symbolically masculine *and* feminine until viewed relative to another tone. The moment two separate notes are sounded together, their vertical relationship as higher and lower pitch values attracts a gender quality. In the language of Western tonal harmony, the *major* intervals, scales, and chords usually relate to the masculine mode, and in contrast, the *minor* key relates to a complimentary feminine mode.

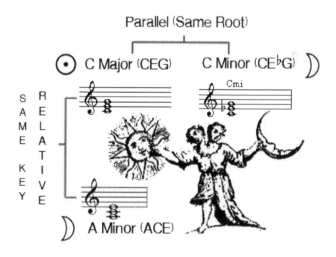

Solar Light of the Major Key	Lunar Light of the Minor Key
Dominant – Active – Positive – Fire Masculine – Dry – Daytime – Heat – Hard – Bright – Ascension – Creative	Passive – Negative – Water – Feminine – Cloudy – Nighttime – Cold – Soft – Dull – Moist – Descent –

C Major Scale

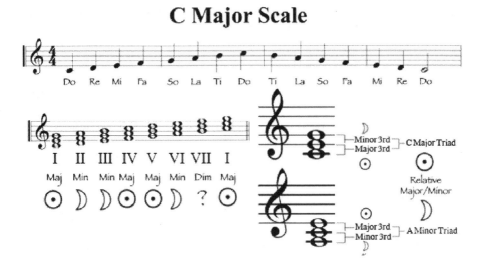

Seven-note diatonic scales can be arranged horizontally in stepwise motion to produce the familiar solfeggio melody, "do-re-mi-fa-sol-la-ti-do". The order of these notes is scrambled up and endowed with rhythm to produce a melody. When these *horizontal melodies* are stacked *vertically,* they form *harmony*, a musical term indicating the sonic relationship between any two or more notes played simultaneously. When three or more notes harmonize together, musicians call the sound a *chord.* Each note of the diatonic scale can be the root of its own chord. A musical key is therefore composed of seven chords: three major chords, three minor chords, and one diminished chord. Chords are combinations of notes derived from the framework of its scalar key signature.

There are strict rules in Western Music around the formation of major and minor chords. Both begin with a foundation of three notes stacked vertically, whose names are the *root, third and fifth.* Their names come from the idea of scale degrees, or position in the diatonic scale, where the triadic chord's root is the *first* note, skipping the second, sounding the *third,* skipping the fourth, and sounding the *fifth.* The interval between root and third in a Major key will always be a major third, while the interval between root and third in a Minor key will always be a minor third. Logically, the names "major third" and "minor third" are derived from this ratio, the relationship between the first and third notes of a major or minor scale. When constructing a musical chord, the major/minor interval relationship between root and third will always be reversed in the interval relationship of third to fifth. For example, a major chord begins with a Root-to-Third interval of a major third and a Third-to-Fifth interval of a minor third. The alchemy of vertical alternation between major and minor thirds is the foundation of Western tonal harmony.

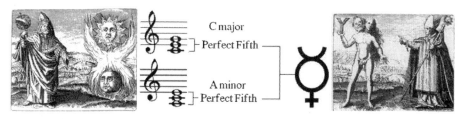

Major and Minor chords share the common root-to-fifth interval of a *perfect fifth*. This is the "power chord" interval, a stable harmony that conveys a sense of containment through which the subtle energies of Sol and Luna can emerge and shine. The perfect fifth interval is featured in both major and minor chords due to the stacking of major and minor thirds as reciprocal opposites. Like the algebraic equation "X+Y=Y+X=Z", one could formulate a similar statement that *"Minor Third + Major Third = Major Third + Minor Third = Perfect Fifth"*.

If we creatively interpret the intervals/scales/keys of music in a way where major corresponds to solar light and minor to the lunar light, then it follows that the perfect fifth ought to have its own alchemical or planetary correlate. In alchemical texts, the union of masculine and feminine is the goal of the great work, and its accomplishment is represented by the figure of Hermes[10]. Bearing in mind that major and minor chords are both composed of two intervals, one major third and one minor third, whose correlates are solar and lunar light, and knowing that the only difference between them is their bottom-up vertical sequence, where major chords ascend from major-to-minor and minor chords ascend from minor-to-major, then the common interval of a perfect fifth in both minor and major chords matches perfectly with the androgynous **Hermes-Mercury** character.

In this knowledge we come full circle to the contemplation of the **88-note piano keyboard as an emblem of Mercury**, whose seven-octave range of 12-tone chromatic scales is first derived from the vertical stacking of fifths, a mercurial and tonally ambiguous interval. This stacking of fifths accounts for only 85 notes, leaving a tiny interval gap of three additional notes, from the highest octave expression of A to C. Synchronistically, or perhaps intentionally, the musical notes A and C are the roots of the two "natural keys", a term that in music theory refers to the major and minor scales

---

[10] It is from the name Hermes that we derive the word *hermaphrodite*, the union of Hermes (messenger of the gods) and Aphrodite (love goddess)

composed of no sharps or flats. A minor and C major are the only two natural, relative keys in the whole musical system. The lowest piano note therefore corresponds to the lunar mode, which has historically been conveyed as subordinate and spiritually "lower" than the sun, while the highest note on the piano corresponds to the solar mode, the superior spiritual force. Their polarity as the lowest and highest points of the spectrum is synthesized by virtue of the other 86 notes of the keyboard. Expressing a full orbit around the sun, the mercurial passage through 88 notes alchemically unites the opposite energies of sun and moon, the projective and reflective manifestations of light. Synthesizing the major and minor triads in terms of the Major-Third-Solar, Minor-Third-Lunar, and Perfect-Fifth-Mercurial intervals, our next task is to integrate the products of those exceptional triads where two minor thirds or two major thirds are stacked upon each other. These triads are known as diminished and augmented chords respectively.

These four chord-types of Major, Minor, Diminished and Augmented represent all the possibilities available from the stacking of thirds in a triad. We have previously identified Major and Minor intervals as having a Solar and Lunar quality. Presented with these two new chord types, we are invited to reformulate and further differentiate these alchemical attributions. For this task we will turn to the four directions, the masculine elements of Fire and Air alongside the feminine elements of Water and Earth.

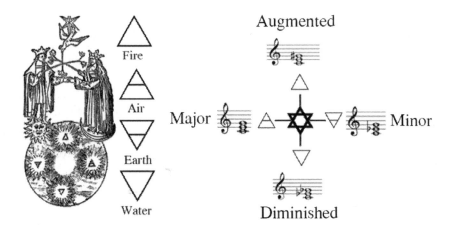

It should be clear enough that the Augmented triad, being composed of two major thirds, would belong to the *masculine* category of elemental energies while the combination of two minor thirds in a Diminished triad belongs to the *feminine*. The classical alchemical symbols associated with each element grant us a clue as to which of the four elements would be attributed to the four triad-chord types. Fire and Water are represented by pure isosceles triangles, whereas a horizontal line intersects those triangles in the symbols for Air and Earth. Symbolically, this suggests that despite their foundation in masculine or feminine energy, Air and Earth are simultaneously composed of their reciprocal opposite. Returning to the musical triads, we can attribute the augmented triad's double-major intervals to the pure ascending isosceles triangle of Fire, the diminished triad's double-minor intervals to the pure descending isosceles triangle of Water, the major+minor interval of a major triad to the bisected ascending isosceles triangle of Air, and the minor+major interval of a minor triad to the bisected descending isosceles triangle of Earth.

Musical Expectation and Planetary Tone-Centers

So far, we've browsed through the basic rudiments of Western music theory. From the 12-tone chromatic scale and layout of the keyboard, we moved into the major and minor scales, along with the seven basic chord triads I-ii-iii-IV-V-vi-vii* and four chord types. The next step in our journey is through chord modulation and how it affects the energetic flow of a piece.

The consonance/dissonance dialectic is a core memetic program of Western music, designed to elicit emotional responses in the audience. Consonant harmonies are stable, complete, and pleasant to the ear, in contrast to dissonance, which is the source of musical tension and restlessness. The play of consonance and dissonance from moment to moment animates the subtle gestures of performance and provides subliminal, emotional context for the listener. Generally speaking, the effect of harmonic tension and resolution produces a unified wave of continuity and contrast.

One common example of this is the tonic-dominant relationship (I-V-I), which shows up in every genre of mainstream western music. *Tonal centers* are like focal points of musical gravity around which the harmonic and melodic development of a piece occurs. When a musician expresses that a song is in the *key* of such and such, they are referring to the tonic, or tonal center. A common technique of Western tonality is to depart from the tonal center in a way that creates a sense of loss and anxiety. The listener longs to hear a return to the center sooner than later, and the composer will periodically return to the home key's root chord as a way of eliciting feelings of comfort and reassurance. Through appropriate preparation and execution, the tonal center can be shifted with the technique of harmonic *modulation*.

Certain chords in a musical key can be modified by as little as one note to create a harmonic tension that tricks the ear and leads it toward a new tonal center. 19th and 20th century composers of the West took modulation to an extreme, developing a chromatic style of songwriting that delayed the return to tonal center for such a long period of time that, if a return ever took place at all, its effect lost much of its meaning. Examples of this can be found in the romanticism of Richard Wagner and the impressionist aesthetic of Maurice Ravel, among countless others.

The shifting of musical modes from one tonal center to another changes the spirit of the tune. By analogy, imagine if the chemistry of our solar system were subject to change over long periods of time, granting life to different planets during different phases of time. In deed, life may have previously existed on other planets in our own solar system[11]. Whenever a planet comes to life, it becomes the tonal center of that solar system for a time. Plants and creatures compatible with the planet's spirit continue to reincarnate for as long as that planet remains the proverbial "home key".

What if there were records of migration and transference of solar consciousness from one planetary node to the next? Equipped with the appropriate inner, psychic technologies of meditation and dreaming, could we in fact glimpse these alternate planetary civilizations? [12] This proposition would seem ridiculous to most people today, but it serves as a perfect analogy for tone center modulation in music.

Earth is home to a smorgasbord of biological organisms that find the planet's conditions agreeable. Imagine these protozoa, bacteria, plants, insects, mycelium, and animals to be hologenic projections of their genetic code. The human species hologram is composed of flesh and blood, the plants of fiber and chlorophyll. Their genetic sequences express fractal micro-iterations of the planet's essence, and the planet in turn is but one facet of the Unity Field. Each planet's electromagnetic field would attract and support a different variety of genetic codes in accordance with its own vibrational nature. The life forms that inhabit a planet contribute in a major way to its identity as a planetary tonal center. We are the biological medium through which a planet dreams its inner essence into materialization.

---

[11] There is a bounty of scientific evidence available in the public arena suggesting that Mars used to be a water-bearing planet capable of supporting life. NASA's Mars rover, the curiosity, has measured a 2% water content in the planet's soil and water erosion is a common feature of its rocks and minerals.

[12] A theosophical expression first coined by Alfred Percy Sinnett, the *akashic record* represents a plane of non-physical existence where everything that has ever happened is stored as if by memory, and as such, can be accessed for the retrieval of information.

Scholars of the ancient world conspired to create a musical system that would awaken the essence of each planetary deity in the listener through the intonation of individual notes. According to legend, each planet is born from a fundamental cosmic template of frequencies, expressing itself in the electromagnetic fields of light and sonic resonance. The planetary *essences*, as nonlocal, subtle and upper-dimensional templates, exert a direct influence through every star system of every galaxy. This concept was formulated explicitly in the magical-musical formulae of the Golden Dawn, which passed through Paul Foster Case into the BOTA and arrived half a century later in this book.

Ceremonial Music and the Occult

The renaissance philosopher and occultist Henri Cornelius Agrippa identified three types of magic, summarized by Gary Tomlinson in his book *Music in Renaissance Magic*. Ceremonial magic represented the passing of wisdom from one generation to the next by way of initiatory rites and the dramatic enactment of carefully orchestrated archetypal situations. Ritual magic drew upon celestial magic for the creation of temple atmosphere. Otherworldly vibrations were invoked and made to appear as if directly from heaven by way of sympathetic images, numbers, geometric shapes, and musical notes, all under the umbrella of planetary domains and their energetic signatures. These celestial magical influences ruled over the heavens, while natural magic, the third category offered by Agrippa, dealt with the manipulation of physical situations on Earth. Initiates were guided through the ceremonial rites of celestial and natural magic, inciting them to discover and come know more about their true nature as spirit incarnate.

Mental perception was framed in terms of syncretic, interconnected webs of sympathetic resonance. Every word, number, and geometric form was imbued with a power derived from its higher, corresponding celestial influence and was harmonized by the logos of divine music. A musical structure that reflected heaven became host to the transcendental influence of the stars. Correspondences between music and the mega-cosmos have been described by occultists throughout history, always within the framework of *sympathetic magic*. Operating on the principle of imitation and sympathetic resonance, this belief system represented an acausal and nonlinear web of interconnectivity almost completely foreign to the modern intellect. Music was regarded by the magician as an audible demonstration of trans-musical, celestial harmonies. Each musical note was distinct and complete unto itself until formulated by stepwise intervals to produce a certain "mode", by which it became part of a larger whole, symbolized by its corresponding astrological bodies. With music as their analog, magicians claimed that all things belonged to an occult harmonic series of sympathy and antipathy - a resonant "key" or mode.

Music played a central role in all ancient initiatory temple rites. Remnants of this can be found in the language of Western Tonal Harmony. Each step along the ascending and descending musical modes is called a *scale degree*. We find this same language in the Hermetic fraternities, especially in Freemasonry, where members ascend stepwise by *degrees* through the ranks of the order. Traditional Freemasonic lodges feature checkerboard *steps* leading up to the altar, to be traversed only by those who have been initiated into the appropriate degrees of knowledge. We can imagine that a similar stepwise ascent by degrees would have been found in the Neo-Platonic magical societies, judging by their representation of the planets as spheres of knowledge whose contents were gradually revealed over time. Each planetary lodge would have featured a corresponding musical mode of stepwise ascending and descending scale degrees, symbolizing the spheres of knowledge available within that Planetary World. We can rest assured that these musical modes were an integral part of the temple's accouterment, alongside the perfume fragrances, gemstones, flowers, fabrics, and so forth. Taken in this context, as an atmospheric accompaniment to centuries old initiatory temple rites, we can see how simple, modal music developed its reputation as a profound metaphysical force in magical societies through the ages.

The mythological and theological roots of music are undeniable, their influence upon actual music composition being occult, intermittent, serendipitous and thus not dependent upon translation. The harmony of the spheres expresses itself through our music without anyone even knowing it. Our collective ignorance of the invisible worlds upon our creative musical acts is not inherently problematic. We can enjoy music without knowing why it influences us in the way that it does. Yet as we discover the mystical roots of music, it seems strange that so little effort has been put toward the overt synthesis of myth and music theory, as if it's a don't-go-there zone in the collective mind field.

The *Don't-Go-There* attitude is always a function of not wanting to see, explore or investigate something that - if brought fully into the light of conscious awareness - would significantly alter or disrupt the conscious sense of ego and identity. When applied to the whole culture at large, "going there" would disrupt the dominant cultural paradigms, and with them the status quo which our hierarchical power structures have selfishly invested in and work perpetually to maintain.

From what I have observed, there is nothing intrusive or disruptive about the integration of mythic content into musical structures and composition techniques, unless those associations become calcified, dogmatic, and absolute. Provided that the meaning of music is allowed to remain a fluid play of empty forms, which is its true and essential nature, we can safely explore the projective, meta-theoretical mapping as proposed in this book and even derive useful interpretations from it. The avoidance of rigid, dogmatic interpretations is of paramount importance! A playful, light and provisional creative approach is definitely encouraged.

The Root of All Creation and Source of the Original Tone

A SONOLUMINESCENT COSMOGENESIS

We discover in astrological and musical models of reality a sound-and-light language that illuminates the abstract realms of human consciousness. Our thoughts and feelings acquire transpersonal context when framed by our Natal and Transit Charts. Drawing upon the Tone Color Alchemy method, we can translate these Heavenly Harmonies into actual musical notes. If we are creative, the planet-sign combinations can be transfigured into melodies, harmonies, and chord progressions that represent psychological forces at play in someone's personal subconscious during a given moment in time.

The events of life on Earth can be viewed as the physical and material embodiments of a higher-dimensional ordering principle. Our foray through the language of astrology represents an attempt to apply these harmonic laws of the human psyche to our personal lives, making them more relevant to us as individuals and helping us to understand how the pieces of our puzzle fit together.

Despite offering deep insights into the nature of human personality, astrology doesn't provide much in the way of a Creation Story. The correlation between Planets, Signs and Houses gives voice to invisible influences upon our personal and transpersonal life experience, but what about the formless consciousness that perceives these influences? How do we account for the mysterious principle of Awareness? This question is an essential part of the Tone Color Alchemy transmission. Let's continue our study by going back even further, transcending the spiritual macro/microcosm of Astromusik through sacred geometric symbols of the Monocosm.

A Syzygy of Ancient Greek and Jewish Metaphysics

Creation stories are ubiquitous among our species. It is as if something in the human psyche longs to understand its origins, and what's more, it would appear that we actually *can* be satiated by the right cosmogenic myths. These stories tend to be, but need not be, theological or mystical in their nature. The Big Bang theory is a scientific cosmology that works for most modern people, and Darwinian philosophy may be seen as the creation story of our species. When we trace the lineage of human cosmology back through time, we discover that peoples' beliefs about the origin of the world did not depend upon the empirical attitude of classical physics or the scientific method. Instead, these versions of reality often maintained that our physical world was an illusion generated by the human senses, obscuring a deeper (upper-dimensional) level of reality where the laws of material existence did not apply. What's more, these higher dimensional spaces were said to begin with a **Creator**.

The *Harmony of the Spheres* was the philosophical foundation upon which the Western world's experiments in music composition were established. It serves as something like a cosmological myth of Music. Yet stories about the Spheres rarely address the cosmogenic act itself. We must turn to religion and philosophy for that.

Pythagoras described the formation of the universe through the symbol of the **ten-sphered tetractys,** the ratios between the spheres symbolizing the interval relationships between planets in our solar system. Likewise, the major archetypal symbol of creation in Jewish Mysticism, the **Tree of Life,** is also composed of **ten spheres**, as described in detail by Jewish Kabbalistic texts like the *Sepher Bahir* and *Sepher Yetzirah*.

Ancient Greek and Jewish philosophies show many similarities. The *Heikhaloth*, for example, was a genre of Jewish esoterica that described the harmony of the spheres as palaces through which the human soul ascends after physical death. The Greek astrological model of music synergizes nicely with this Kabbalistic philosophy, while remaining individual in its employment of unique symbols and stories. To understand how these two philosophical lineages overlap, we will turn to the work of **Paul Foster Case** and **David Allen Hulse,** two modern scholars of the occult who have penetrated the Kabbalistic mysteries of creation and codified them in an elegant geometric progression hinted at by the Sepher Yetzirah. Later in this book I will elaborate upon the historical context for this cosmogenic model, but for now let us stay the course, drawing upon visual aids and the written word to transmit the essential message of this story.

3-Dimensional Euclidean Space and the Cube of Creation

According to conventional wisdom, all physical bodies can be identified by their location in a time-space matrix, described according to qualities they display *locally.* For example, as I write this paragraph, my body is located in a small independent coffee shop in the Pacific Northwest. You can measure my height, weight, and various other physical characteristics quantitatively only once you have knowledge of my true location. How could you measure me if you don't know where I am? Furthermore, the subtle and relatively "subjective" levels of emotional and intellectual activity channeled through my body are inseparable from the physical organism that receives and transmits them. For this reason, a simple model for identifying the location of a body in space proves invaluable to our developing knowledge and understanding of a "thing" as it exists in the World.

One of the earliest efforts to talk about spatial location was championed by the Greek philosopher and mathematician *Euclid of Alexandria.* He promoted the belief that perpendicular intersecting planes generated what we today would call the X, Y, and Z axes of a 3-Dimensional cube. Objects could be pinned to the intersection point between polarities of Up-Down, Left-Right, and Forward-Backward. Euclid defined each of these poles as belonging to one of the six faces on a cube. The intersection point between X, Y, and Z axes defined the center of the cube and the spatial "location" of a thing. Within this model of space, time could be represented as a one-dimensional track upon which the cube travels, like a railway, moving perpetually from past to future with the center of the cube representing the always-present moment and sacred NOW.

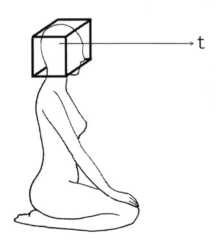

As mentioned earlier, the general tendency of metaphysics is to attribute a higher order of reality to the mundane world, a model of life independent from the conventional ideas of physical locality in space-time. In Buddhism, time has in some instances been represented by a necklace of cubic beads - symbols of the moment-by-moment creation and destruction of reality. When we become absorbed and attached to the phenomenal world of these successive moments, we get lost in an illusion. Only the thread passing through the necklace can be said to have real existence, as representation of the unchanging and continuous flow of energy that unites all moments.

The conventional, theoretical notion of time portrays a constantly changing zero-dimensional point defined by the intersecting influences of info traveling along the X, Y, and Z axes of our perceptual cube. Time is defined by our perception of changes in spatial events. Viewing time this way, we collapse a 4+Dimensional reality into the conventional 4-dimensional space-time world model, effectively casting a spell upon our own perceptions, causing "time" to appear as either Zero-dimensional (Now-Moment) or One-Dimensional and linear (Past Present Future).

What would it look like to entertain a 2-Dimensional representation of the 4+Dimensional reality? What geometric forms would be most accurate and how could these maps of higher dimensions deepen our appreciation for simple. everyday life? What facets of existence would they illuminate that the zero/one-dimensional maps of time do not already reveal?

Jose Arguelles, founder of the Planet Art Network, portrayed time in terms of interconnected cycles of change, which he called the **Synchronic Order**. To the strict chronologist, it makes no sense to talk about overlapping timelines of a synchronic order from the 4-dimensional model, because these coinciding moments would amount to physical collisions. For example, if I am at the center of my cube of space and my timeline intersects with yours, our bodies would literally crash and merge into a shared zero-point. Physical collision is clearly not the intended meaning of synchronicity. Instead, the synchronic order seems to be pointing at the ***co-incidental resonance of meaning,*** rather than the simultaneous occupation of physical space by two or more objects. The synchronic order presents a map of overlapping *archetypal forces.* Therefore, synchronic time would have to be defined by something other than one's perception of changing events. Physical events would be re-contextualized as ***effects*** of a higher, trans-physical and formative plane of existence - the 4+Dimensional Time Domain.

Zero-Dimensional and One-Dimensional Models of Time

CHRONOS AND KAIROS

The Pre-Socratic Greek philosophers conjured special god forms to represent their notions of linear time and the present-moment. On the one hand, Chronos, from whom we get the word *chronological*, represented cycles of time and was personified in the Orphic poems as a winged three-headed serpent. Snakes have long been used as symbols of time, in Egyptian myths for example, because of their biological inclination to be reborn through the shedding of skin. Chronos was later identified as Saturn in the Roman cosmology, wherein he was depicted as an old man with a long grey beard, also known as **Grandfather Time.**

On the other hand, there was the Greek God Kairos who represented a kind of *special time,* in contrast to the quotidian (daily and annual) time cycles of Chronos. Kairos-time was conceived of as an absorption in the present moment. His name suggests the idea of a time-lapse and a supreme moment defined by its *qualities* rather than a measurement of chronological *quantities*. A group of prominent Greek philosophers during the 5th century B.C., called Sophists because of their veneration of Sophia, Goddess of Wisdom, made Kairos a central element of their teachings. Each moment was viewed as a unique opportunity for the adept to skillfully adapt to life's circumstances. The Sophists spoke of *prepon* and *dynaton,* which translate to English as the *appropriate* and the *possible*. In relation to Kairos, these modes of intelligence suggest a **wise response to each moment**. Generally speaking, Kairos represents the idea of a critical moment in time, a meaningful opportunity, and the wisdom of an individual to respond to life appropriately.

Returning to the aforementioned Euclidean space-cube, we can correlate these two deities of Time to the geometric polarity between the cube's **center** as a **zero-dimensional point** (Kairos) and the **timeline** as a **one-dimensional track** upon which the cube travels sequentially from **past to future** (Chronos). The intelligence of Kairos comes directly from the Creative Spirit (God) and transcends mere response-abilities to chronological time. Kairos relates to the idea of our human heart as a *Zero-Point portal into 4+Dimensional time zone.* The upper-dimensional representations of time can hardly be called "time" at all, as they defy our most basic assumptions about time as being a linear sequence measured by physical phenomena.

Stepping Through the Zero-Point Star Gate into 4+D

The Western mind tends to think of physicality as a way of gauging truth. If something can't be measured in terms of physical events in the material world, then it's not real, and if it's not real, it's hardly worth our attention. This is precisely why atheism and the rejections of metaphysics have become so common in our culture. The western mind has turned a blind eye to magical thinking. Conventional education, materialism and territorial power grabbing have reinforced our antipoetic attitudes. Nevertheless, stories continue to convey meaningful insights that enhance our experience of life on Earth. Music and movies provide something for the post-modern individual that religion rarely can. They put people in touch with transpersonal patterns of mind that permeate the collective unconscious, reminding us of our connection to universals encoded within the human condition. Art has the power to heal one's attachment to carnal life, poking fun at habitual tendencies and occasionally hinting at a deeper divinity dwelling within.

The Zero-Dimensional point at the center of the Cube of Space can be viewed as a black hole of one-pointed awareness and perception. When we embody the energy of Kairos through a dynamic outwardly-receptive relationship to the faces of the cube, we can feel things happening all around us and learn to take advantage of what is available in the moment so as to manifest desired outcomes. However, Kairos also invites a second option of *introversion,* whereby we pull away from the outer world and drop through the zero-point rabbit-hole of qualitative perceptions into Timelessness. We will be spat out the other side into a 4+dimensional synchronic order (syn: together, chronos: time) where all sense of linearity and physicality dissolves into a continuity of higher dimensional templates and formative influences. This is the world of astrological and alchemical archetypes and the place where Greek philosophers sought the fabled Harmony of the Spheres. It is also the meta-physical and sacred domain described by Jewish kabbalists in texts like the Sepher Yetzirah.

The ideas presented are intended as a poetic and intuitive summary of ideas hinted at by Case and Hulse in their writings on the Cube of Space, Tree of Life, and the Tarot. The cube in question has two primary roles; first as a three-Dimensional Euclidian model of physical space, and second, as the **Qabalistic Cube**, which represents a *meta-physical* map of archetypes dwelling in 4+Dimensional space. The Qabalistic cube was first described in detail by the **Sepher Yetzirah**, a concise magical treatise written somewhere between the 1st and 9th century A.D., attributed to the biblical character Abraham. The contents of the Sepher Yetzirah emerged from a long line of kabalistic secrecy and oral tradition. We can assume that its attribution to Abraham is a testament to the traditional nature of the teachings and was intended to mask the identity of its actual scribe. We see the same kind of anonymous mysticism in Greek, Egyptian and Arabic metaphysics, one obvious example being *the Emerald Tablet of Hermes Trismegistus*. It is common in this field that heroes of the Imaginal Realm are credited with writing texts that couldn't possibly have been written and published by their physical person - not within the framework of our classical understanding of reality, anyway.

We don't need to know who wrote the Sepher Yetzirah to enjoy and employ its contents. The book describes a number of beautiful correspondences between the Hebrew alphabet and astrological archetypes. These teachings gradually found their way into the late 19th century initiatory rites of the Hermetic Order of the Golden Dawn, and in turn, to the early 20th century tarot studies of Paul Foster Case. Case was one of the first to publically disclose a chain of relationships between the alphabet, the kabalistic tree of life, and the cube of space. He points out in his book *Tarot: A Key to the Wisdom of the Ages* that the 22 letters of the Hebrew alphabet map onto the 22 components of the cube.

The logic of this connection is elucidated by the Sepher Yetzirah in its visual depiction of the Rose, a three-phase unfolding of Hebrew letters beginning with three mother letters at the center of the flower, followed by seven double letters in the middle layer, and twelve simple letters along the outer layer. The 22-sum progression from **three to seven to twelve** is identical with the Cube, whose X, Y, and Z axes correspond to the three mother letters, whose six faces plus center corresponding to the seven double letters, and whose twelve edges correspond to the twelve simple letters. Furthermore, these twenty-two letters and components of the cube map onto another Kabalistic diagram called the Tree of Life. This tree is composed of 10 spheres and 22 paths between the spheres. David Allen Hulse, author of *New Dimensions for the Cube of Space*, demonstrates how the **ten spheres** relate to the cube, while allowing the **twenty-two paths** between those spheres to share in these same attributions.

At first this system may seem technically challenging and even obtuse, yet over time one comes to recognize the incredible simplicity and elegance of its structure. Because this is a book on the application of Qabalistic magick to musical divination, I hasten to add that the 22 paths correspond also to the 12 notes of the chromatic musical scale. A familiarity with this system can open us up to new techniques of navigating the psyche and composing music. These compositional methods will soon become evident.

Cube of Space to Kabbalistic Rose to Kabbalistic Tree

The 4+ Dimensional Model of Creation

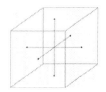 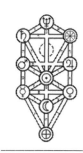

X+Y+Z axis = 3	Mother Letters = 3	
6 Faces + Center = 7	Double Letters = 7	
Twelve Edges = 12	Simple Letters = 12	

Total Number of Aspects = 22	Total Number of Letters = 22	Total Number of Paths = 22
Cube of Space	Kabbalistic Rose	Kabbalistic Tree Of Life

As you can see, the rose described by the Sepher Yetzirah features a single letter on each petal. The philosophy behind this sacred symbol can be understood in simple terms: **God created our physical reality through an original word**. The Hebrew language was a gift from God within which he encoded the logos of his Divine Genius. Each letter is qualitatively different, in the same way that the elements of the cube are geometrically distinct from one another. Just as the cube unites its twenty-two aspects into one form, the Hebrew alphabet accomplishes this very same thing. As a unified field, the twenty-two letters of the alphabet co-inform each other and can be artfully combined by way of the alchemy of language. I would direct the curious reader toward Both Paul Foster Case and David Allen Hulse for further information. These authors offer a detailed account of the relationship between the letters and the cube, along with initiation into the imagery of the major arcana.

A re-appropriation of the 22 letters from the Cube of Space to the Tree of Life allows us to completely snap out of the abstract, 3-Dimensional Euclidean space of the cube and begin approaching the Kabbalistic sacred geometric model of cosmogenesis. The geometry of the Tree of Life is derived from the Flower of Life, which in turn comes from the Seed of Life, and as you will see, can be traced all the way back to the original and primordial state of **total emptiness** which is the **source of our creative potential**. Before we venture toward the Flower of life, we will pause on the Tree and review each of the letters, contemplating their unique qualities within this tradition. As I have already established, the attributions of each letter come through magical correspondences taught by Paul Foster Case and the Hermetic Order of the Golden Dawn.

The Kabbalistic Tree of Life

In the mystical Judaism of Kabbalah, the Tree of Life is considered to be a central image and symbol of the Inner Planes. Composed of ten visible spheres and one invisible sphere, interconnected by way of the twenty-two paths, this Tree represents the whole cosmogenic process, from the original spark of life at the top of the tree to the final physical-material manifestation in its lowest sphere. The biblical story about the Garden of Eden refers to a Tree of Life and a Tree of Knowledge of Good and Evil. Both of these trees in Eden are represented by this same symbol, viewed from two different perspectives. A part of the Jewish faith for millennia, the Tree was integrated into mystical Christianity and hermetic alchemy during the European Renaissance. It has since become a centerpiece in the initiatory rites of Western ceremonial magick, each sphere representing a degree of initiation.

The ten spheres are said to represent ten distinct realms of experience. In the ceremonial traditions of the Golden Dawn and B.O.T.A. they correspond to the celestial spheres. The lowest sphere is called Malkuth and corresponds to Earth, divided into the four elements of Earth Air Water and Fire. Ascending from Malkuth, the initiate passes through the sphere of Yesod (Moon), Hod (Mercury), Netzach (Venus), Tiphareth (Sun), Geburah (Mars), Chesed (Jupiter), Binah (Saturn), Chokmah (12 Signs), and Kether (Neptune). In this way, the "spheres" of the Tree of Life literally correspond to the Greek notion of the **Harmony of the Spheres**, the 22 paths connecting them symbolizing the celestial harmony *between* those Spheres.

Curiously, the paths themselves do not represent musical intervals, as one might expect given the idea of a "harmony of the spheres". Each path represents only one musical note, along with a single color, a single tarot card, a single Hebrew letter, and even a planetary/zodiacal attribution. Therefore, the "harmony" referred to by the Tree is not a function of multiple musical notes being played simultaneously, but instead, a multiplicity of individual sacred symbols ascribed to the path itself. [13]

In contrast to the 4-D time-cube, the Tree of Life's 4+D dimensional map of the Synchronic Order describes *qualities*. They intersect symbolically because the 22 aspects of the cube **(3+7+12)** map onto the 22 paths of the Tree. The 10 spheres of the Tree, then, represent trans-dimensional time nodes merging distinct paths of spiritual experience. The 22 paths correspond to the 22 cards of the tarot's major arcana, each path

---

[13] A detailed account of attributions to the paths is given multiple times throughout this book. See *Figure 1* on page 67 for details.

corresponding to one card, while the minor arcana, or playing cards (ace through ten), map onto the ten spheres of the Tree. The four suits of the cards, as well as the four royal cards in each suit (page, knight, queen and king), relate to the *Four Kabbalistic Worlds*. An image of the four worlds is provided on the next page. They stack vertically and reiterate the same ten celestial symbols through the four elemental modes, representing our emanation from the original condition of Spirit toward the manifestation of physicality.

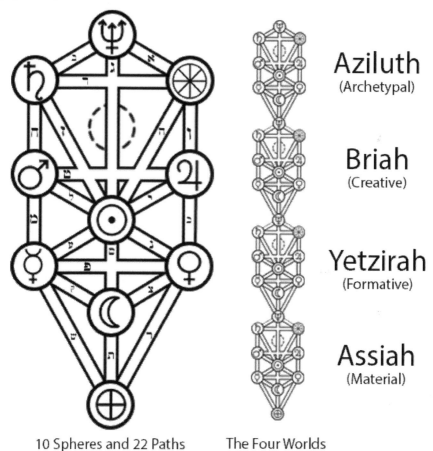

10 Spheres and 22 Paths   The Four Worlds

Aziluth
(Archetypal)

Briah
(Creative)

Yetzirah
(Formative)

Assiah
(Material)

The twenty-two Hebrew letters and their inner meanings, as described in the following pages, each map onto one of the twenty-two paths of the tree. As one would come to expect by now, the **attributions** of letters to the tree **differ between each lineage**, so that in some traditions, the paths have a completely different set of associations and may not even have planetary attributions to the spheres at all.

GEMATRIA AND THE HEBREW ALPHABET

HEBREW	TONE COLOR	ASTROLOGICAL	GEMATRIA
Aleph	E Yellow	Uranus	1
Beth	E Yellow	Mercury	2
Gimel	G# Blue	Moon	3
Daleth	D Green	Venus	4
Heh	C Red	Aries	5
Vav	C# Red-Orange	Taurus	6
Zayin	D Orange	Gemini	7
Cheth	D# Orange-Yellow	Cancer	8
Teth	E Yellow	Leo	9
Yod	F Yellow-Green	Virgo	10
Kaph	A# Violet	Jupiter	20
Lamed	F# Green	Libra	30
Mem	G# Blue	Neptune	40
Nun	G Blue-Green	Scorpio	50
Samekh	G# Blue	Sagittarius	60
Ayin	A Blue-Violet	Capricorn	70
Peh	C Red	Mars	80
Tzaddik	A# Violet	Aquarius	90
Qoph	B Violet-Red	Pisces	100
Resh	D Orange	Sun	200
Shin	C Red	Pluto	300
Tav	A Blue-Violet	Saturn	400

Kabbalistic Correspondence Table

The twenty-two letters of the Hebrew alphabet correspond to the 10 planets and 12 signs perfectly by way of their attributions onto the Tree of Life and Cube of Space.

Prior to the invention and integration of Arabic numerals, Jewish and Greek letter alphabets doubled as their number systems. Each letter had a numerical value. In Hebrew, the translation of letters into numbers was called gematria. These alphanumeric codes play a critical role in Western Ceremonial Magick today.

Sacred Breath

Aleph

Tone-Color:	E Natural – Yellow
Letter Symbolism:	Ox / Bull
Tarot Card:	The Fool
Gematria Value:	I
Astrology:	Uranus
Tree of Life Path:	Path II from Kether to Chokmah

Qabalistic Significance

Aleph is the first letter in the Hebrew alphabet (Greek: Alpha) and is spelled אלפ {ALP}. The gematria value of these three letters add up to one hundred and eleven {A:1 + L:30 + P:80 = ALP:111} symbolizing a sacred trinity of unities encoded into the threefold shape of the letter itself. Rotating the letter so that its central line is vertical, the shape of aleph can be projected onto the upper half of the human spine so that its two appendages overlap with the lungs. It has been written that **Aleph** represents wind, air and the **breath that animates all life.**

As the first letter of the alphabet, Aleph shares in the nature of Kether, the first sphere on the tree of life, a symbol of the original spark of Creative Consciousness. Aleph corresponds to the Crown Chakra in the human nervous system; yet given its threefold nature, this letter also aligns with the supernal triad of Kether, Chokmah and Binah. In kabalistic lore, this triad represents the closest thing to the Christian idea of a holy trinity, or the Hindu *trimurti* of Brahma, Vishnu and Shiva.

Aleph's affinity with the air element can be visualized in a number of ways. Specifically, its shape resembles a swastika, which prior to its use by the Nazis was a nearly universal symbol for solar radiance. When rotated a full 360-degrees on its central axis, Aleph assumes the form of a windmill or fan-blade. This spinning letter represents a pure seed of consciousness residing at the center of a circle (Kether) extending through two alternate channels (Chokmah/Binah). Stirring up empty space and generating an energetic hurricane, Aleph's gyration *generates its own energy* rather depending on an external energy source. Accordingly, it would appear that Aleph resembles what in quantum physics would be called a *self-excited circuit*.

Unlike the English alphabet, where letters are more or less autonomous, lacking any explicit "meaning" separate from their role in the construction of words, each letter of the Hebrew alphabet carries a corresponding word-meaning. The letter A (Aleph) means Ox, the letter L (Lamed) means Ox-Goad, and final letter P (Peh) means Mouth. Thus the primordial power source of creation symbolized by the Ox (Aleph) is provoked into circulation by the Ox-Goad or Cattle Prod (Lamed), by way of the respiratory system of the lungs, extending its influence to the Mouth (Peh) to produce the original Divine Word. The first two letters of Aleph (ALP) are AL, which in Hebrew can be pronounced "El" translating to English as "Lord". The idea of a **sacred word**, as in the quote from John 1:1, "In the beginning was the word, and the word was with God, and the word was God," can be interpreted as an **invocation of Aleph**.

Ancient Egyptian and Hindu reverence toward the *apis bull* or *sacred cow* relates closely to this meditation. Ox-drawn carts were historically used to plow the field, increasing crop production and relieving farmers of certain hard, physical labors. The strength of a single ox transcends the strength of many human beings, much like the transcendental strength of God. In the sacrificial rites of archaic fertility cults, the Persian Mithraic Mysteries being a prime example, bulls were often ritually slaughtered to confer an empowerment, bathing initiates in blood and putting them directly in touch with the spiritual strength of the animal's spirit. Life-force energy and perseverance are closely related to the vital Winds of Aleph.

House of God

Beth

Tone-Color:	E Natural – Yellow
Letter Symbolism:	House
Tarot Card:	The Magician
Gematria Value:	2
Astrology:	Mercury
Tree of Life Path:	Path 12 from Kether to Binah

Qabalistic Significance

Beth is the second letter of the alphabet (Greek: Beta) and is spelled בית {BYT}. The shape of the letter represents a floor, wall, and roof, and the letter when spelled out phonetically creates the word BYT which means "**house**" or tent. The first line of the Old Testament (Genesis 1:1) opens with the word בראשית (*Bereishit*), which means **Creation** or **Genesis**. Look closely and you will see that the first and last two letters of this word form Beth {בית}, bookends of the letters ראש {ROSh} which translate from Hebrew to English as **King**. Thus בראשית is linked to the idea of a King's House (**House of God**). Alternatively, the letter Beth ב can be distinguished from the other letters ראשית {RAShEeT: **Kingdom**} to produce a second meaning. Beth is the second letter of the alphabet, so it implies **duality** or two-ness, and combined with the Hebrew word for kingdom, it implies the idea of **Two Kingdoms** (Macrocosm/Microcosm). Created in God's image, Beth represents both our Physical and Spiritual Bodies.

Our bodies are likened to a temple, housing the indwelling Spirit of Creator. There are certain mantras in Tibetan Buddhism designed to empty the practitioner of their attachment to forms, so that there is no longer anything to defend. They use the analogy of a thief entering an *empty house*; nothing can be stolen and nothing can be lost, therefore the problem is resolved before it even begins. We can imagine that our Ego is like this thief, wanting to gratify innumerable desires and therefore incurring karmic debts. Grasping at the pleasures of life makes it difficult to receive the grace of God, which truly is the highest source of pleasure. God will not enter a filthy temple. Therefore, cleansing our soul of desire and attachment is essential if we wish to come fully into harmony with the Divine.

The inspirited **body**, represented by Beth, is considered by kabbalists to be a feminine counterpart to the masculine **spirit** of Aleph. Together they form the word אב {AB: Father} suggesting that the **Father** is androgynous and double-gendered. Corresponding to this second alphabet letter (Beth) is the second sphere of the tree of life (Chokmah) whose meaning is **Wisdom** and which corresponds to the Gnostic image of Christ as the **Son of the Father**. As a symbol of our sacred imagination, Christ is the avenue through which we come to experience the ineffable essence of his Father. All our perceptions are filtered through the sacred imagination. To clean up the contents and activities of our imagination is to make space for the influence of Aleph, pure life-force energy, allowing God's grace to descend upon our physical body and bestow unspeakable spiritual treasures.

Visually, the floor and foundation of the letter Beth ב relates to the ninth sphere of the tree of life, Yesod, ruled by the moon and having to do with sexuality and astral travel. Through purifying the sexual channels in our body we transform the images and energies coursing through our imagination. Sexuality is closely related to creativity, our personal body-temple being the direct result of our parent's sexual relationship. In the imagery of the tarot, Beth corresponds to the Magician card, depicting a human body serving as vessel and channel for Spirit's descent from the canopy of roses to the garden of roses and lilies. Modern occultists, diverging from the chaste traditions of Jewish kabbalah, have correlated Beth to the secret art of **sex magick**.

Holy Spirit

Gimel

ג

Tone-Color:	G Sharp - Blue
Letter Symbolism:	Camel / Heavy Rope
Tarot Card:	The High Priestess
Gematria Value:	3
Astrology:	Moon
Tree of Life Path:	Path 13 from Kether to Tiphareth

Qabalistic Significance

Gimel is the third letter of the Hebrew alphabet (Greek: Gamma) and is spelled גמל {GML}. The phonetic spelling of this letter creates the word **Camel (gaw-mal)**. There is a famous biblical aphorism from the book of Matthew 19:21-24, where Christ says to his disciples "Again I say to you, it is easier for a camel to go through the eye of a needle than for a rich man to enter the kingdom of God." This cryptic statement has been turned over and contemplated from multiple angles. What is the meaning of a camel passing through a needle?

To better understand this riddle, we turn to the history of the text. There is strong evidence that the New Testament was initially written in a combination of Aramaic and Hebrew. The Aramaic translation of the word GML is **Heavy Rope (ga-ma-la)**. When we substitute this idea for the camel, the metaphor makes more sense. The only way a thick rope could fit through the eye of a needle would by its unraveling into individual threads. It follows that Christ was teaching the importance of unraveling our identity and relaxing our attachment to the things of this world.

As the third alphabet letter, gimel may be interpreted in relation to Binah, the third sphere on the tree of life. Binah represents the Supernal Mother and our capacity for **Understanding**. Gimel **stands under the foundation** of the House (Beth ‎ב‎) the way a camel stands under and supports its human passenger, the House of God. Its underneath-ness suggests the physical-material world of matter (Latin: mater = mother). The word substance (sub: under | stance: stand) brings us closer still to the meaning of Gimel. It implies the embodiment of a spiritual essence subordinate to a higher influence.

As the path from Kether to Tiphareth, representing the crown and heart chakras respectively, gimel provides a direct vertical channel across what Qabalists refer to as the Abyss, the gap between the supernal triad and the other seven spheres on the tree of life. Many have written about the Abyss as a desert that must be crossed by the initiate. Traveling upon the path of gimel suggest a journey across the desert via camelback. In the B.O.T.A. tarot attributions, gimel corresponds to the High Priestess and the Moon. The camel's **crescent-shaped** hump is a fat depository that metabolically transmutes fat into **water** and **energy** over the course of its journey across the desert. This is the secret of its perseverance. Note the similarity to candle wax (the fat) and candle wick (gimel = rope).

Gimel as a thick rope also relates to the idea of the human spine. A well-known Kabbalistic text called the Zohar ($2^{nd}/13^{th}$ century) explains, *"When the angel Samael tempted Adam to eat of the tree of knowledge of good and evil, he was riding a camel-like serpent ... which means that the camel and the serpent that delivered death to the world are the same thing."* If gimel is taken as a symbol of the spinal column, its connection to the serpent may have to do with kundalini energy (sexual fire). In desert dwelling civilizations, the camel implies mobility of trade and commerce, accumulation of wealth, and the temptations of worldly life, including sex and sensory pleasures.

Paul Foster Case attributes Gimel to Chokmah rather than Binah, pointing out that both GML {G3+M40+L30=73} and ChKMH {Ch8+K20+M40+H5=73} add up to 73.

The Door

Daleth

ד

Tone-Color:	F Sharp - Green
Letter Symbolism:	Doorway
Tarot Card:	The Empress
Gematria Value:	4
Astrology:	Venus
Tree of Life Path:	Path 14 from Binah to Chokmah

Qabalistic Significance

The previous commentary on Gimel describes its passage across the Abyss, from Kether to Tiphareth. As the fourth letter of this alphabet, Daleth (דלת) corresponds to the hidden sphere, Da'ath (דעת), positioned at the center of the Abyss and corresponding to the throat chakra. Coincidentally, a letter-for-letter translation of דעת would be **DOT**, connecting to the idea of gimel passing through the **eye of the needle** to reach God. In Hebrew, the word Daleth means Door, its shape (ד) resembling the letter Beth (ב: House). Taken in its biblical context, the letter D appears significantly as the middle letter of both the name Adam (אדם) and Eden (עדן). Daleth has been framed as the *door* through which Adam and Eve left Eden. The proverbial garden is synonymous with the kingdom of heaven, symbolized by the supernal triad, with the path of Daleth connecting Chokmah to Binah to create the bottom line of that supernal triangle.

Crossing the abyss from Tiphareth to Kether entails crossing over Da'ath and Daleth, both of which bear close similarity to an English homophone; the word *Death*. While Daleth corresponds in tarot to the Empress card and the idea of the sacred yoni, our doorway into the world, it also represents our doorway *out of the world* through disincarnation. This dual-direction quality of doorways relates to Daleth's gematria value of 4 (2x2) suggesting our movements in life from in-to-out and out-to-in, our entrance and exit from life. Da'ath has been called the sphere of Knowledge, suggesting that our passage between worlds may lead to attainment of special knowledge. Consider this in the context of the Near-Death and Out of Body experiences cited in the earlier chapter on the Harmony of the Spheres. We bring back knowledge of the astral realms from our journey across the Abyss.

Our human senses are the doorway through which energy manifests in consciousness as recognizable forms (knowledge). In Hebrew, the first two letters of Daleth form the word Dal (דל) meaning "poor". In contrast to gimel, which represents substance and wealth, Daleth traditionally represents spiritual and material poverty. Yet without the poverty of Daleth, Gimel would have no meaning, and so the word God (GD: גד) represents the union of spiritual wealth with material poverty. This relates to the image of yogis and renunciates who turn away from the world in order to develop a relationship with G-D. In Hebrew, Gad (גד) means "to say", implying the creative and cosmogenic word. The word was with God and the word *was* God גד.

There is a close relationship between the tree of knowledge, serpents, and sexuality. Eden is the world of pleasure and bliss. As the path connecting the Supernal Father (Chokmah) and Supernal Mother (Binah), Daleth symbolizes sexual union and delightful experiences that open up the **Doors of Perception**. Where Beth represents the body, as a symbol of House and temple, Da'ath as a Door represents the exchange of sacred fluids between partners. Here there is a close connection to the astrological sign Scorpio, which corresponds to the Death card in the tarot and symbolizes the intense, conjoined influences of sex and death, the Greek gods *Thanatos* and *Eros*.

Thought Speech and Action

Heh

Tone-Color:	C - Red
Letter Symbolism:	Window
Tarot Card:	The Emperor
Gematria Value:	5
Astrology:	Aries
Tree of Life Path:	Path 15 from Chokmah to Tiphareth

Qabalistic Significance

Where Daleth represents the door to a House (Beth), Heh represents a wind-door, or window, through which the Emperor looks out upon the kingdom. You can detect this in the space between the wall and roof on the left column of the letter. Paul Foster Case attributes **Vision** to Heh, explaining that the Spirit calls the universe into existence through seeing and contemplating its own true nature.

The 2x2 movement symbolized by passing in and out through Daleth (the door) echoes in the symbolism of Heh, the **winds** represented by both **Aleph** (Sacred Breath) and **Yod** (Sacred Fire) via their mutual resonance with Kether. Heh is a major element of Tetragrammaton, the unspeakable four-lettered name of God, spelled YHVH (יהוה) translating to the familiar names Yahweh and Jehovah. The absence of consonants in the former name brings it closer to the true and intended pronunciation. Heh represents an open throat through which the vowel sound of Yod (divine spark) connects with Vav (the spine) to activate and circulate kundalini energy through the body.

As the second letter of the Tetragrammaton, Heh resonates with the feminine-receptive qualities of Binah. In Hebrew, the placement of Heh at the end of a word implies a feminine form. As the fourth letter of Tetragrammaton, it relates to the final stage of manifestation and the Kabbalistic world of Assiah. It may be spelled הה adding up to 10 (5+5) and therefore also resonates with Malkuth, the tenth and lowest sphere on the Tree of Life.

The tenth letter of the alphabet is Yod י (God's Hand) that splits up into the left and right hemispheres, five fingers per hand, to create הה (H+H=5+5=10=Yod). We shape the elements of Malkuth with our hands, receiving and deriving their creative power from Yod, the Divinity within, reinforcing the image of Heh as a door through which the power of God (Kether) passes to effect change in the world.

An alternative spelling of Heh is הא (HA) implying a window through which the Sacred Breath of Aleph passes. Aleph (1) is the reduced form of Yod (10=1+0=1) and is imbued with its creative power. Heh in this instance represents our vocal folds, which physiologically resemble the female genitalia. In this feminine attribution, Heh connects to the **uterus** and has been called the throat of God. Genesis describes the creation of the world through speech. Our World is made up of many little worlds; the creation of the Universe and the creation of a single Human Being are isomorphic.

When in Genesis 47:23 Joseph says "Lo, take seed for you, and ye shall sow the land", the first word, Lo, spelled הא, is intended to attract our attention. The merger of Heh (Uterus) and Aleph (Life Force) in relation to the Seed (Z'RA: זרע) suggests pranayama and the use of breath to circulate sexual energy. In English the words Heh (הה) and HA (הא) both suggest laughter, while AH suggests understanding and contentment. Over the millennia, these primal sounds have retained their traditional attributions of Joy and Divine Revelations: the sacred AH-HA moment! ABRAHADABRA!

The Spinal Column

Vav

Tone-Color:	C Sharp – Red-Orange
Letter Symbolism:	Nail
Tarot Card:	The Hierophant
Gematria Value:	6
Astrology:	Taurus
Tree of Life Path:	Path 16 from Chokmah to Chesed

Qabalistic Significance

This letter plays an important role in Hebrew and the Torah. As the third letter in the Tetragrammaton YHVH (יהוה) it represents the passage of life force energy from God to Creation. A majority of the sentences in the first five chapters of the Old Testament (the Pentateuch) begin with the letter Vav. In Hebrew it means **Nail**, but also doubles as the word "and", so that each sentence is symbolically nailed in conjunction to the previous one. When the Tetragrammaton is mapped onto the middle pillar from top to bottom, Yod corresponds to Kether (Crown) and the first Heh to Da'ath (Throat) so that **Vav corresponds to Tiphareth** (Solar Plexus) and the final Heh to Yesod (Sacral Chakra).

Resonating with Vav, Tiphareth's central location is the **"and"** of the Tree of Life, connecting **to all six spheres** of the **Left and Right Pillars of the Tree**, and linking vertically with Da'ath and Yesod, the intermediaries to Kether and Malkuth.

A great deal of sexual meaning is attributed to Vav in the context of YHVH. It links the above (YH) with the below (second H) as the union of mind and sex organs. The fiery waters of the Shekinah, the Divine Mother, which come down from Upper Eden (Kether) to redeem Lower Eden (Malkuth) can only do so by way of a clear channel. Through sexual misconduct we obstruct the flow of energy along our spine, hinted at by the biblical passage *"For your transgressions was your mother put away."* (Yeshayah 50:1).

In the story of Moses's visit to the Pharaoh's court, he threw his wooden staff upon the floor and transformed it into a serpent. Vav represents the spine, symbolized by its straight, vertical shape. The thirty-three vertebrate of the spinal column correspond to Vav through gematria (33=3+3=6). Totaling 33 degrees of initiation, each vertebrate has its own essence and energetic quality. Vav can be pronounced as a hard V or soft U/W, implying the flexibility of our spine as well as the soft and erect forms of the phallus.

Recall that the first two letters of Aleph (AL) means Lord in Hebrew. The Zohar describes in detail the sacred marriage between masculine and feminine energies as Eloah (אלוה), where Heh ה and Vav ו represent the feminine and masculine sex organs respectively, and AL אל represents the presence of God in that marriage of opposites. Enclosed is a teaching on the art of raising our serpent energy along the rod of Vav, the androgynous skeletal support column that is our spine. As a transducer of spiritual light, and because of its correspondence to Tiphareth, the solar center of the Tree of Life, Vav and the spinal column become symbols of the human soul.

Creative energy channeled through the body amplifies our power to manifest change in the world. The Hebrew word *avah* {AVH: אוה} is a verb that means "to wish". It adds up to 12 (5+6+1), which is the sum of Vav when spelled out (VV: 6+6=12). Consider this in relation to the healing staff of Hermes-Mercury, the Caduceus, or the healing rod of Asclepius. Both of these relate to vav and avah, the fulfillment of wishes coming through us by way of the grace of God. This is the staff held by the Hierophant in the major arcana, its sexual meaning indispensable to the teachings that he imparts upon the abbots.

Double-Edged Tongue

Zayin

Tone-Color:	D – Orange
Letter Symbolism:	Sword
Tarot Card:	The Lovers
Gematria Value:	7
Astrology:	Gemini
Tree of Life Path:	Path 17 from Binah to Tiphareth

Qabalistic Significance

Whereas the sum of Gimel (GML: 3+40+30=73) resonates with the sphere of Chokmah (ChKMH: 8+40+20+5=73), the sum of the letter Zayin (ZIN ז'ן: 7+10+50=67) resonates with the sphere of Binah (BINH בינה: 2+10+50+5=67). Chokmah and Binah represent the Supernal Father and Mother on the Kabbalistic tree of life, as opposite poles of the Supernal Triad. Have you noticed that G is the third letter in both Greek and Hebrew alphabets (gimel/gamma), whereas it is the seventh letter in the English alphabet? Zayin is the seventh letter in the Hebrew alphabet and gimel the third. According to historical records, the Roman censor Appius Claudius purged the letter Z from its position as the seventh letter, replacing it with the letter G, making C the third letter instead. *In music theory this coincidence takes on further meaning, as the key of C Major is called the natural key (it has no sharps or flats). The dominant chord in relation to C Major is G major. G wants to resolve down to C. The two of these exist in dynamic tension and opposition to one another.*

The word Zayin זין means sword in Hebrew. As the seventh letter it relates to the division of Time (ZMN: זמן) into seven parts, such as the Shabbat (seventh day of the week), the Shavu'ot (seventh day of seventh week after Passover), Tishri (seventh month of the year), the Shemitah (seventh year), etc. The number seven thus represents both the intellectual separation of wholeness into separate parts as well as a period of rest during completion of a cycle. Zayin connects in this way to Binah, which Qabalistically is ruled by Saturn, lord of Time.

In some instances Zayin may literally refer to a weapon, though in other instances the idea of a sword is used metaphorically. Take for instance the biblical quote from Revelations 1:16 referring to the Son of Man: *"In his right hand he held **seven stars**, from his mouth came a **sharp two-edged sword**, and his face was like the sun shining in full strength."* Where we would expect to find a sword, the Son of Man instead carries seven stars. The sword dwells in his mouth, indicating the attribution of Zayin to Gemini (the sign of communication).

Our tongue dwells *above* in the moist cavern of the mouth. Notice the visual similarity between Zayin ז and Vav ו and recall that Vav symbolizes both the spine and phallus. Zayin has been called a "crowned Vav" because of their subtle differences in shape. The tongue is positioned at the top of the spine and can be soft or erect like the phallus as symbolized by Vav. Zayin dwells in the mouth, upper Eden, corresponding to the female genitalia in lower Eden. In this way, the tongue lives in a wet feminine environment, in contrast to the relatively dry and masculine environment of the phallus.

Rabbi Baal Shem Tov famously said that a woman of virtue was the crown of her husband, alluding to the mystery of Zayin. In this case it refers to the head of Zayin (yod) as the seventh chakra and the pineal gland. The fiery waters of Binah circulate through this gland and are bound to the circulation of sexual energy in Yesod (The Lower Dan-Tien in Taoist alchemy). Through a sublimation of our kundalini energy (inward and upward ejaculation), our Vav-spine unites with the Yod-crown to produce Zayin. This is a primary secret of sexual transmutation.

The Inner Self

Cheth

Tone-Color:	D Sharp – Orange-Yellow
Letter Symbolism:	Fence
Tarot Card:	The Chariot
Gematria Value:	8
Astrology:	Cancer
Tree of Life Path:	Path 18 from Binah to Geburah

Qabalistic Significance

The Hebrew word for life, Chai (חי), shows up in the kabbalistic idea of Nephesh Chayah (נפש חיה) or the "living soul". In contrast to the letter Heh, whose shape represents a window, the letter Cheth is closed on both sides and when spelled out (חית) means "fence". The window has been sealed to produce a closed container, i.e. the temple. The gematria value of the word חית is 418 (8+10+400) shared by the magical formula ABRAHADABRA (418 = 1+2+200+1+5+1+4+1+2+200+1). There is something dark and mysterious about this letter, perhaps due to its connection with enclosed spaces and secrecy. As the letter corresponding astrologically to Cancer, the Crab, Cheth represents our inner life and our protective shells. Surrounding the tree of life is *Ain Soph Aur* in three layers. The latter two words (סעפ אור) Soph Aur mean "Limited Light" and add up to 418 (60+70+80 plus 1+6+200). Yet Soph also means Wisdom, as in the Greek goddess Sophia, and so the limited light does not necessarily have a "negative" meaning.

The uppermost horizontal line of Cheth symbolically bridges the gap between the left and right pillars of the Tree of Life. If Zayin were attributed to the left pillar and Vav to the right, then Cheth would represent the synthesis of those two letters, the twin forces of Mercy and Severity. The whole Tree is enclosed within the temple of Cheth, with Yod (Kether) at its roof and Malkuth at its root. The three central spheres that remain, Yesod, Tiphareth, and Da'at, represent the foundation, heart, and throat of God.

We unite the essence of Zayin (woman) and Vav (man) to create a child. It is a traditional Jewish custom, as illustrated in the Zohar, that on the eighth day after birth, the mother and father are obligated to circumcise their baby. As the eighth letter, Cheth is like the foreskin of a phallus, protecting it from exposure to the light, keeping it in darkness. There is a word in Hebrew, Chattah (חטאת), which also adds up to 418, and which means *sin* or *punishment*. The ultimate sin in this lineage would be to turn away from God in service to the dark, "lower" animal nature. Cutting away foreskin symbolizes the removal of one's animal desires and a purification of the soul.

It is this author's opinion that circumcision, as an act of genital mutilation, is a cruel and abusive relic of the past. It literally scars the phallus and potentially scars the child's psyche. I do not agree with the Kabbalistic perspective that the animal nature needs to be cut away, but rather, I propose that we embrace our so-called lower and primal nature and learn to integrate it as part of our person.

From the traditional view, the removal of Cheth leads to liberation. By removing the boundary (fence/walls) between our body and the totality that envelops it, we come face to face with Ain Soph Aur, the limitless light. What began as a primordial fear of the darkness and as defenses against the Outside eventually will become an expansive attitude toward the unity of God's Creation. This relates closely to the moment of death when our soul is liberated from its chariot, the body, and reconnects with its source. In a similar way, it speaks to the spiritual rapture of sexual union between a man and woman, where the boundaries are eliminated and lovers merge as one, symbolized by Crowley's famous aphorism 2=0 & 418 = ABRAHADABRA, the "Reward of Ra Hoor Kuit" (AL III:1)

Kundalini / Sexual Energy

Teth

מ

Tone-Color:	E - Yellow
Letter Symbolism:	Serpent
Tarot Card:	Strength
Gematria Value:	9
Astrology:	Leo
Tree of Life Path:	Path 19 from Chesed to Geburah

Qabalistic Significance

We correlate this ninth letter of the alphabet, Teth, to the ninth sphere on the Tree of Life, Yesod, which represents the Foundation of the Great Work and corresponds to the lower Dan-Tien, an energetic point about two finger-widths in and below our belly's navel. Recall the familiar image of a cobra curled up in a basket, summoned by its master, the snake charmer. One flute song can be enough to draw it up and out of its coiled slumber. The spelling of Yesod (יסוד) is similar to the Hebrew letter Yod (יוד), the only difference being its inclusion of the letter Samekh (ס). Compare the ninth letter Teth and fifteenth letter Samekh (ט and ס) and you will see the similarity between them. Teth represents a serpent wrapping in towards itself, its face coming inches away from its tail, whereas Samekh represents the ouroboros snake that bites down upon its tail. Do you see how Samekh ס forms a circular ring with Yod at the top? In ancient Hebrew the symbol of Samekh *was* the symbol for Teth, thus the relationship between Samekh, Yod and Teth is important.

Recall from the meditation upon Cheth that three rings envelop the Tree of Life. They are its nest as well as its life and sustenance. From these three layers, called Ain Soph Aur (No-Limit-Light or Limitless Light), comes the original sphere and crown of the Tree of Life, Kether. At the center of these three circles is the Hebrew letter Yod. The shape of Yod is present in all 22 letters of the alphabet, a design element that implies the omnipresence of God and the influence of Kether upon all spheres and paths of the Qabalistic Tree. Yod is the core essence of Ain Soph Aur distilled in particle form. The heat generated by this spinning ouroboros, which is the self-sustaining serpent power of the Universe, is mirrored by the center as a flame.

In the major arcana of the tarot, the key images of Magician (Beth) and Strength (Teth) share a tone color (E-Yellow). **The Magician wears an ouroboros around his waist like a belt,** implying a Yod at the center of that area of his body, which is precisely where we would find the sphere of Yesod. Both the man in the magician card and the woman of Strength wear a lemniscate, or figure eight, hovering above their head. This symbol of infinity is a variation on the serpent-circle, twisting in upon itself self-referentially. In the Strength card we see a woman gently holding open the mouth of a lion. **Leo's tail conceals the serpent power of Teth.**

There is another letter "T" in the Hebrew alphabet, Tav, which in ancient Hebrew was represented by a circle with a cross at its center. The Phoenician letter *Tet* is shaped in this very way and means "wheel", connecting Teth again to the circle, this time as the Wheel of Fortune and the Wheel of Samsara (Reincarnation). **It was a serpent in the Garden of Eden that tempted Eve to taste of the forbidden fruit.** Upon doing so she and Adam lost the privilege of immortality and stepped onto the wheel of rebirth. Teth ט unites Vav and Zayin by way of Yesod, the foundation, where the **coiled sexual energy of our kundalini serpent** resides.

Eve ate from the **Tree of Knowledge,** discovering the **art of sexual alchemy,** in contrast to the Kabbalistic tree of life, the intellectual alchemy of Hebrew Letters. These two trees offer co-informative elements of initiation into our Higher Self, the lower and upper Eden.

Universal Flame of Consciousness

Yod

י

Tone-Color:	F – Yellow-Green
Letter Symbolism:	Hand
Tarot Card:	The Hermit
Gematria Value:	10
Astrology:	Virgo
Tree of Life Path:	Path 20 from Chesed to Tiphareth

Qabalistic Significance

A great deal can be said about the letter Yod. Its Hebrew meaning is **Hand** and its shape may actually be formed by pressing the thumb and forefinger of one hand against the forefinger and thumb of the other, creating a rectangle. When you apply some pressure, the rectangle bends and morphs into a Yod י. This relates to the previous meditation on Teth and Samekh, where Yod represents the fiery energy at the center of a rectangle (samekh ס), corresponding to the dot at the center of Kether. The formula 10=1+0=1 and the abbreviated name of God as JA (יא) hint to Yod's attribution as the first sphere on the Tree, Kether, rather than the tenth sphere, Malkuth. Of course, encoded in the ONE is the potential realization of the TEN and vice versa. As above, so below. Both spellings of Yod (יד / יוד) imply the passing of this Hand of God through the Door (Daleth ד) into Existence. Our ten fingers are doorways through which Yod's fiery and creative energies may pass into the elemental world of Malkuth.

Paul Case refers in his *Book of Tokens* to ancient pictographs of Yod as a pointing finger. In Michelangelo's famous painting, the *Creation of Adam*, Yod is suggested by the tiny gap between the pointing fingers of Man and God. Another name for the Tree of Life is Adam Kadmon, thus the Creation of Adam is analogous to the Creation of the Tree of Life. Yod may also be translated from Hebrew as "Arm", representing humanity's reaching out toward God in prayer. The arm, hand and fingers are all extensions or appendages of Adam Kadmon, the spiritual torso of Man as symbolized by the Tree of Life.

Yod יוד begins with a point (Yod י) extending down (Vav ו) and then to the left (Daleth ד), thus with the seed letter Yod we derive the vertical and horizontal planes of 2-D geometry with which we make our Tree. William Blake famously asserted that "Art is the Tree of Life, Science is the Tree of Death". His negative representation of YHVH (יהוה) as the demiurge **Urizen** (*Grand Architect and Geometer*) amounts to a rejection and demonization of the reasoning tendencies of Mind, in contrast to the Imagination, which Blake held in the highest reverence. This psychological polarity between the left and right hemispheres of the brain is mirrored in the Pillars of the Tree.

Correlating to the English letters Y and I, the vowel sound of Yod is pronounced "eee" and when intoned causes the skull to vibrate, stimulating the pineal gland and opening up our Kether (Crown). Imagine you are gazing at the profile of a person who faces to the left. The left surface of Yod י can represent the face of that person when in prayer, the up-turning tip of Yod suggesting the ascending energy of the third eye as it comes up and out through the forehead, while its lower-right tip bends in submission and reaches down vertically, hinting at the spinal column of Vav (ו). Yod is like the eye at the center of a Hamsa (an upside down hand that serves as protective amulet and talisman throughout the Middle East). The gematria value of Yod when spelled יוד (10+6+4) has a sum of 20, the same as the word *Chazah* (חזה: 8+7+5=20), which means "*to see*" and may also refer to a prophet. From this we come to understand that Yod's omnipotent influence makes it the source of all prophetic visions. With Yod, our Divine Spirit, we each create and recall all perceptions.

The Golden Cap

Kaph

Tone-Color:	B Flat - Violet
Letter Symbolism:	Palm of the Hand
Tarot Card:	The Wheel of Fortune
Gematria Value:	20
Astrology:	Jupiter
Tree of Life Path:	Path 21 from Chesed to Netzach

Qabalistic Significance

This letter closely resembles the second letter of the alphabet, Beth, the difference being that Kaph is made from one brush stroke rather than two. If you compare their shapes by flipping between the two meditations, you will see how the foundation of Beth protrudes slightly from the bottom right of the letter. With a gematria value of 20, Kaph reduces (20=2+0=2) to Beth.

The word Yod יוד means "hand" whereas the word Kaph כף means "palm", referring to the energetic focal point of the hand. Kaph may also translate into Hebrew as "spoon", contributing to the image of the palm as a shallow container. With a gematria value of 20, twice that of Yod, it suggests the sum of toes and fingers and has been symbolized by the word Kafah (כפה) which means to bend over, invert, or overturn, as reaching down to grab the feet with one's hands. In doing so we form a little cup (Kaph) with our body in the space between our arms and legs.

Kaph's spoon-like quality has also been traditionally associated to the King's Crown, because of the little container created along the inner rim of the crown. Connecting with one's own spiritual crown (Kether: KTR כתר) requires concentration and discipline (KVNH כונה). Kether, the crown of the Tree of Life, begins with the letter Kaph for a reason. Remember that Aleph is the first path to emerge from Kether and that in Hebrew, Aleph means "Ox". Perhaps it is a coincidence that the word Kaph in English is a homonym of the word Calf. We are reminded of the biblical story of Moses and the false idol of the Golden Calf. YHVH forbids the creation and worship of images, whereas many other desert dwelling cultures during the early history of the Jewish people were actively worshipping the bull and making a sacrifice of the animal in their prayers to the Creator. After the Israelite's incident with the golden calf, the priests were forbidden to wear golden crowns. Instead it was taught that they should wear the crown of Torah and the crown of a good reputation.

The familiar Yiddish word yarmulke (pronounced yah-ma-ka) is called a kippa (כפה) in Hebrew and is a **spoon-shaped cap** (kaph) worn upon the head. It takes the place of a more ornate, golden crown, yet it signifies something similar. Orthodox Judaism demands that the religious authorities wear a cap at all times, whereas others are expected to wear it only during prayer. It serves as a reminder of the inner Yod at the center of the head, as if spooning the skull.

Christ spent his last moments on earth in crucifixion, the palms of his hands and the soles of his feet (both symbolized by Kaph) nailed to the cross and his head crowned with thorns. As the number 20 symbolizing the sum of fingers and toes, Kaph is related to the act of combining the energy centers (palms and soles) so as to amplify and direct that energy toward different areas of the body. To cross one's hands over the chest in an X represents the resurrection of Osiris in the ritual work of the Golden Dawn, signifying the sublimation of sexual energy from the root and sacral centers to the heart. As the 11th letter in the alphabet, Kaph corresponds to the uniting of the pentagram (5) and hexagram (6), symbols of body and spirit, therefore this symbol has to do with the achievement of bringing the kundalini energy up from the base to the crown of the spine.

The Heart of the Mind

Lamed

ל

Tone-Color:	F Sharp - Green
Letter Symbolism:	Cattle-Prod (Ox-Goad)
Tarot Card:	Justice
Gematria Value:	30
Astrology:	Libra
Tree of Life Path:	Path 22 from Gevurah to Tiphareth

Qabalistic Significance

Kaph represents the palm of God cupping the crown of our physical head. **Lamed** inverts this gesture, the yod shape at the upper left part of the letter signifying a line of energy that comes up and out from our forehead like a *hand* reaching toward Creator. This part of Lamed has been called the Flying Tower. The three letters Kaph, Lamed and Yod combine in the word *keli* (כלי), which in Hebrew means *vessel*. Drawing from Kaph, symbolizing the union of below and above, Lamed pulls energy up from the heart and expresses it out through the flame of the mind's eye, Yod. Therefore our heart, symbolized by Lamed, is the vessel of energy transfer between Yesod and Kether. In the Tone Color Alchemy system, Lamed corresponds to Green, which is the center of the rainbow spectrum (ROYGBIV). In its correspondence to Libra, Lamed represents the Justice card, depicting a woman on a throne holding a sword in one hand and balancing scales in the other, just above her heart. As the eleventh letter, Lamed is the heart center of the Hebrew alphabet.

With the sword in her right hand, the justice character cuts away falsehood and goads the initiate forward along the path. Lamed means "sting", "poke", and "jab" implying a forceful gesture, and in some cases an authority figure. In ancient times, shepherds would corral their animals with a staff and in some biblical passages, the word *lamad* means to "teach" (Deuteronomy 4:1 for example). We are guided toward right knowledge by way of the heart, lamed. The Hebrew word for heart is spelled Lamed Beth (לב) and pronounced *lev,* a homophone of the English word *love.* When we get off track from our life's purpose, the heart suffers and attempts to redirect us, prodding us lovingly towards the attainment of a more balanced state of mind, speech and action.

The word לב adds up to 32 (30+2) and corresponds to the thirty-two paths on the Tree of Life; the sum of its ten spheres and twenty-two paths. To know the true nature of each path we must meditate upon them, perhaps at first beginning with intellectual ideas about the Tree, but eventually emptying our mind of all thoughts and feelings, dissociating from our body and allowing our soul to journey through the higher-dimensional planes of energetic essences. A similar word to lev is *lebhabh,* spelled LBB (לבב), translating to English as the heart of the mind. It symbolizes the solar radiance of the physical heart dwelling within our brain, observing the perpetual thoughts and feelings that we call Mind. Spiritual lib-eration is not found in the **lab-yrinth** of mental ideas and beliefs. Awareness, symbolized by lebhabh, is the true heart of the mind that shepherds our thoughts and purifies the intent behind our actions.

Imagine that the shape of Lamed traces the profile of a seated person facing toward the right. The upper left Yod shape comes out the back of their head, the vertical staff representing their spine (Vav), the horizontal line representing their foundation (Yesod) and the final semi-diagonal line representing their legs tucked slightly under the seat. This describes a meditation posture that one can comfortably hold for long periods of time so as to achieve deep contemplation. Consider the 6,200 page collection of meditations upon the Torah, the books of the Talmud (תלמוד) whose name combines the letter-words Tav (תו) and Lamed (למד), uniting **World** with **Heart.**

Creative Waters

Mem

Tone-Color:	G Sharp - Blue
Letter Symbolism:	Water
Tarot Card:	Hanged Man
Gematria Value:	40
Astrology:	Neptune
Tree of Life Path:	Path 23 from Gevurah to Hod

Qabalistic Significance

Mem represents the deep mysteries of **water** in all of its symbolic permutations: streams of consciousness, ocean waters, fountains of youth, amniotic fluids of the womb, and undulating waveforms. It is spelled without a vowel in the middle (MM: מם) and could thus be pronounced "Mom" in English, though as "Mem" it also connects to the English words **memory** and **remember**. The reflective qualities of water make it an apt symbol for the **Mind**, which takes information from sense perceptions and presents it to consciousness in a way that resembles a mirror. Think about a mirage in the desert. Our mind presents consciousness with convincing illusions, and on occasion may even misrepresent reality, the way that a lake may reflect the trees and sky of the landscape without actually taking on any of its physical characteristics. White noise generated by rolling rivers similarly can produce auditory hallucinations. One may feel convinced that they hear music simultaneous with the rushing water, only to discover that it was all in their head.

Mem has two visual forms, one closed ם and one open מ. The first is called *stumah* and represents the hidden truth of God, whereas the open form, *pesucha*, is a symbol of divine revelation. In its open form, Mem looks like a Vav ו (6) conjoined to Kaph כ (20) with a small gap between them at the bottom left of the letter. Their sum as 26 corresponds to the Tetragrammaton YHVH (יהוה = 26) and in this way the open Mem visually depicts the four-lettered name of God. The letters Yod and Vav, both present in YHVH, combine with the letter Mem to form the word **Yom** (YVM: יום), which means day, **Yam** (YM: ים) which means ocean, and **Mayim** (MYM: מים) which means water. These words do not only refer to the physical ocean waters or literal days defined by the sun cycle. In the very first line of genesis, when we see the phrase "In the beginning God created the Heaven and the Earth," the word Heaven is spelled *Hashamayim* (השמים) and in the second line, when "The spirit of God moved upon the face of the waters", water is spelled המים.

Water is essential to the creation and maintenance of all living bodies on Earth. The shape of open Mem represents a woman's birth canal, by which the waters of life bring us into this world. In Hebrew the Divine Mother, *Aima* (אימה), is associated with the third sphere on the tree of life, Binah, who in turn draws her divinity from Ain Soph, the cosmic egg that envelopes and supports the Tree of Life. Another name for the Divine Mother is *Miriam* (מרים), the Hebrew name of both Moses's sister and Jesus Christ's mother, Mary. The Zohar refers to Miriam as the chariot of the *Shechinah*, the healing waters of God.

It was similarly said about Christ, in John 7:38 that "Out of his heart will flow the rivers of living water," a symbol of what is promised when we have faith in God. Faith is a necessary component because as the open and closed forms of Mem elucidate, the presence of God reveals itself to the heart while remaining closed off to the reasoning faculties of the intellect. Faith represents a trust in the heart and a willingness to surrender our need to mentally understand something. Thus in the tarot, Mem corresponds to the Hanged Man suspended from the cross, and to Neptune, the Greek god of the ocean.

Sperm and Seed

Nun

נ

Tone-Color:	G – Blue-Green
Letter Symbolism:	Fish
Tarot Card:	Death
Gematria Value:	50
Astrology:	Scorpio
Tree of Life Path:	Path 24 from Tiphareth to Netzach

Qabalistic Significance

The fish lives and thrives in an aquatic environment, and so it is that Nun could not exist without the previous letter, Mem. When the two combine together we get the English word **Man**, which in Hebrew is spelled מנ and pronounced *manna*. In the biblical Book of Numbers, the Israelites are starving and complaining that they miss the fish that they used to eat in Egypt. God responds by granting them manna, a seed-like resin that came when the dew settled on the camp at night. The Jews dried and ground up this manna in a mortar, turning it into loaves of bread. In the New Testament, Christ famously performed "the miracle of the seven loaves and fish," turning to heaven with a prayer that some 4,000 starving people would be fed. Breaking a loaf of bread in half and circulating it through the crowd, Christ was able to feed thousands of people with what seemed to be only a meager portion. Christ was the harbinger of the astrological age of Pisces, the fish, and during the Christian ritual of the Eucharist, one eats a piece of bread symbolizing the body of Christ, the spiritual food (manna) of initiates.

Mem, as a symbol of womb water, supports and nourishes the life force energy embodied by Nun, the manna (sperm) of a man. The combined gematria values of Mem and Nun is 90, a numeric value shared by the Hebrew word Melech (מלכ: 40+30+20=90), which translates to English as **King**. Geometrically, the number 90 signifies the degrees of right angle created by the intersection of vertical and horizontal planes in the crucifix. The cross, like the hexagram, represents the meeting of spiritual and material layers of reality.

Nun is shaped like the right half of Mem, illustrating that it is part of a bigger picture. The Hebrew word for river is *nahar* (נהר) connecting to the idea that Nun is but a tributary of the cosmic ocean. Like a river pouring out from the sea, the animal element of the human soul, called the Nephesh (נפש) in Kabbalah, represents the part of us that longs to reunite with its intrinsic wholeness. The animal part of the soul comes from God but is not synonymous with God. Yet the animal is not separate from God either. Psychologists talk about this in terms of a concept called the Ego-Self axis. During prayer, we may speak *to* God as if he/she/it were separate from us. In some ways this is helpful. But is a river truly separate from the ocean out of which it emerges? And what happens to a fish out of water?

In the major arcana of the tarot, Nun corresponds to the Death card. How can it be that this symbol of life force energy would come to be associated with Death? Behind the skeletal grim reaper is a rising sun, signifying that the vitality of Nun brings resurrection and salvation to that which is dead. With a gematria value of 50, Nun connects to the idea of the first day after completing a seven-week cycle (7x7=49). However, the Hebrew word *naphal* (נפל) means failure and Nun (נ) in some instances implies degeneration or suffering. During the end of his physical incarnation, Christ cried out "My God, my God, why have you forsaken me?" indicating his deep sense of abandonment. According to the Gnostic worldview, Christ's suffering was not in vain. With his death, he repaid the karmic debts of all sentient beings. The Zohar writes that in the word Amen (אמנ) we invoke the breath of God (א), inseminate the Waters of Creation (מ) and produce the magical child (נ). Encoded in this word *Amen* is the whole creative act.

Unlimited Power

Samekh

Tone-Color:	G Sharp - Blue
Letter Symbolism:	Prop
Tarot Card:	Temperance
Gematria Value:	60
Astrology:	Sagittarius
Tree of Life Path:	Path 25 from Tiphareth to Yesod

Qabalistic Significance

The full circle shape of Samekh was said by the *Chazal*, a historical body of Jewish sages during the 2nd century B.C. through 6th century A.D., to be representative of the eternal spiral ascent of God's grace and glory. Samekh is the first letter of the Hebrew word *Seder* (סדר), a ritual feast marking the beginning of the High Holiday of Passover, which is itself a yearly and therefore *cyclical* recounting of the Israelite's liberation from slavery in Egypt. When Samekh is spelled out as a word (סמכ) it means, "to support". In the pragmatic sense, samekh may refer to an architectural prop, such as a tent pole, yet like most words found in the bible, it has multiple metaphorical correlates and alternative uses. The *sukkah* (סוכה) for example, is a temporary *tent* built during a week long festival that celebrates God's *support for his creation* and provision for the needs of his chosen people. Being a transient structure, the sukkah symbolically reminds the Jewish people of their ancestor's transient existence in the desert, the transience of human life in general, and dependence upon God.

A priestly blessing called the *Birkat Kohanim* is found in the biblical book of Numbers (6:23-27) composed of 60 letters and 15 words. As the fifteenth letter of the Hebrew alphabet with a gematria value of sixty, Samekh resonates with the *blessing power of the righteous*. When we open ourselves to God with perfect faith and trust, miracles become possible. The Hebrew word for miracle is *nes* (נס) beginning with the partial and bent quality of Nun (letter-shape) and finding completion in the circular quality of Samekh. One returns from a broken state to a sense of wholeness and completion by way of God's miracles. *Nes* also refers to the sail of a boat, suggesting that we are carried forward along our life path by the winds of Spirit. A priest's blessings similarly come from a power greater than their person; the Aleph of God moves through them and is the true source of all miracles.

Aleph is like a spiritual windmill, sent into circulation through devotion and prayer to God. The circular shape generated by its rotation implies Samekh, the serpent swallowing its own tail, and as the first letter of Soph (סוף) from the Kabbalistic *Ain Soph Aur*, it plays an important role in the crystallization of Kether and the whole Tree of Life. The serpent power of Soph is evident in the Hebrew spelling of the word. Vav has been correlated to the spine and Peh to the mouth, therefore samekh as the ouroboros serpent relates to the coiled energies ס at the base of the spine ו that rise through the central energy channel and find expression through songs of praise and worship פ.

Recall that the Hebrew letter Teth ט means *serpent* and corresponds to the snakelike tail of Leo, the true source of the lion's power. As a solar creature, the lion draws upon the serpent's sexual potency and expresses it through proud displays of dominance over the rest of the animal kingdom. Our sun is similar in its visibility and dominance over the solar system. Both draw their energy from what **Samekh** represents, the cumulative cycling of energy through a closed circuit. The timeless nature of Source-Consciousness (God) renders it immensely powerful, because there is no creation or destruction of energy. All the energy that ever has been and ever will be is available here and now provided that we are living in right relationship to the Creator.

Consciousness in the World

Ayin

Tone-Color:	A – Blue-Violet
Letter Symbolism:	Eye
Tarot Card:	The Devil
Gematria Value:	70
Astrology:	Capricorn
Tree of Life Path:	Path 26 from Tiphareth to Hod

Qabalistic Significance

Represented by the tarot card "The Devil", traditional attributions to Ayin are split, representing both the powers of light and darkness. As the outcome of the two previous letters, Nun and Samekh, and their mutual influence in the Hebrew word *Nes*, meaning "miracles", Ayin represents the direction and application of God's blessing power in the world. Our willful application of consciousness, represented by Ayin, can steer life in whatever direction we choose. When spelled out (AYN: עין) it means "eye" and implies the power of vision. It may refer to the physical organ of the eye, but more importantly to Kabbalah, it evokes the idea of a second-sight or what Castaneda called the **second attention**, the ability to place our awareness upon the spirit world of dreams and psychic visions. When we view and perceive the world through the **evil eye**, Kabbalists says that we become enslaved to sinful impulses, as in the word *aveira* (עבירה), for "transgressions" against man and God, whereas the **good eye** leads to good deeds and service, represented by the Hebrew word *avodeh* (עבבדה).

With our physical eye we look out upon the world and receive light. Our inner eye translates the sensations of our organ into the perceptions of our mind. The *ayin tovah*, or good eye, is a code word for the personality that responds to the world with charity and good will, whereas the *ayin hara*, or evil eye, is consumed by greed and envy, seeking to fulfill only its own insatiable desires. When we speak of God's all seeing eye as an omnipresent awareness, we refer not to a passive observer but rather to an involved participant that sustains and supports its creation. The devil represents the dark half of God, the part that supports and sustains those who cultivate the *ayin hara* and brings suffering to the righteous.

In Hebrew the word Tree is *otz* (עץ), from which we get the names for the Tree of Life (עץ החיים) and Tree of Knowledge (עץ הדעת טוב ורע). The eleventh and hidden sphere of the Tree of Life, called Da'at, is spelled דעת and implies a door through which one sees the world. It is called the sphere of knowledge because one must truly *see* if they wish to know God. It is not enough to have theoretical knowledge. We rely on direct experience, what the Greeks called Gnosis, for clairvoyant perceptions of the life on Earth. The light of Ayin, which illuminates our Tree of Life and Knowledge, determines what we can see of our own true nature and in the world around us.

Introspection is a function of Ayin turning back upon itself, in a way, to the inner life of perceptions. With our inner Eye we discover the inner "I" or ego-identity which is both the source and consequence of that balance between light and dark within us. When we choose to see the world in a negative light, we accumulate negative thought forms that congregate in our psyche and become the foundation of our identity. When with the inner vision we shed light upon our own darkness, we gradually liberate ourselves from bondage to the Devil and attain the Good Eye.

Here it is important to point out that in Ayin's shape, the split between the Left and Right paths (evil and goodness) stem from the same source. These two organs belong to the same head, and to recognize this is to achieve salvation, *ozer* (עזר), from duality. Our shadow and evil aspects are a byproduct of our Divinity and Light.

Creative and Destructive Power of the Word

Peh

Tone-Color:	C - Red
Letter Symbolism:	Mouth
Tarot Card:	The Tower
Gematria Value:	80
Astrology:	Mars
Tree of Life Path:	Path 27 from Hod to Netzach

Qabalistic Significance

Who speaks? What good is a mouth without sentient consciousness to animate it through vocalization and meaningful communication? The Eye of Awareness, represented by Ayin, perceives reality and transfigures the signal according to its personal ethics. A response to the outside world comes not through the inner workings of the eye alone. We must complete the feedback loop of perception by way of **Peh**, the **mouth**, whose Hebrew meaning is also "word" and "speech", signifying creative output through the mouth. This is true in ordinary, everyday conversation, in the sense that we shape and influence the world according to the way we relate to it, how we see it and what we say about it. The creative power of Peh and the mouth also applies at the level of cosmogenesis, illustrated by the aphorism that "In the Beginning was the Word". Interestingly, the gematria value of Peh is 80, the same value indicated by the spheres of Yesod (Foundation: יסוד) and Geburah (Strength: גבורה) on the Tree of Life, and so we may come to understand that **Peh** is the **foundation** of our **strength**.

The Tower card of the tarot's major arcana is completely sympathetic to the meaning of Peh as *mouth*. It shows a lightning bolt striking the tower of Babel and two people falling from its heights, containing multiple esoteric meanings. Genesis 11:1-9 describes how "The whole earth was of one language and of one speech". A group of people had found an open plain of land to settle. They said "Come, let us build a city and a tower with its top in heaven and let us make a name". Having accomplished this intention, they attracted the attention of God who came down and said "Behold, they are one people and they have all one language ... and now nothing will be withholden from them which they purpose to do", implying that their unity of speech had created a comm-unity of great strength. How does God respond?

"Come, lets us go down, and there confound their language that they may not understand one another's speech."

The lightning bolt featured in the imagery of the Tower represents God's superior strength to the collective will of the people. It is strange that in the biblical passage on Babel, God speaks as "us", implying a multiplicity of gods. That opens a whole can of worms. Is God a symbol for a multiplicity of extraterrestrials, i.e. embodied entities living off-planet with superior intelligence to humankind, monitoring and "playing God" with us? Why would they wish to disturb our unified effort to build a tower that reaches up to heaven? It seems as if the creative word of God in the opening lines of Genesis represents a different agency than the God described in the story of Babel. The Tower card correlates to the planet Mars, the god of War.

An alternate version of the tarot from the 17th century depicts the Tower card as "**The Lightning**", striking a tree rather than a tower. What happens when we take the Tower of Babel as a metaphor for the Tree of Life? The B.O.T.A. deck subtly illustrates the lightning bolt as a passage of energy from Kether to Malkuth, zigzagging through the tree and touching the center of each sphere. The shape of the bolt implies the Tree, and its destructive impact upon the tower seems to suggest humanity's attempt to reach God through artificial constructs as being doomed from the very beginning. Only our nervous system, as an organic emanation of the Creative Spirit, has the structural integrity to receive and withstand the Will of God.

Compassion as Sustenance

Tzadik

Tone-Color:	B flat - Violet
Letter Symbolism:	Fish-Hook
Tarot Card:	The Star
Gematria Value:	90
Astrology:	Aquarius
Tree of Life Path:	Path 28 from Netzach to Yesod

Qabalistic Significance

The spelling of Tzadik (צדיק) relates closely to the word Tzod (צוד) that in Hebrew means "to capture". The shape of the letter itself resembles a **fishhook** and this is one of Tzadik's commonly attributed meanings. Built from a bent letter Nun, whose Hebrew meaning is "**fish**", and the letter Yod, which means "**hand**", Tzadik may be interpreted as the attaining of one's sustenance, symbolized by catching a fish. Our previous meditation upon Nun established it as a symbol of the body of Christ, and so the second common meaning of Tzadik as "righteous one" corresponds to the idea of a servant of God who reaches up with their hand to heaven, a sign of humility and surrender. When the 16th century Rabbi Isaac Luria described the movement from Ain Soph Aur to Kether as a willful contraction (*tzimtzum:* צמצום) from infinitude to singularity, he correlated this to the tzadikim, who humbly make themselves less so as to make others more. One example of this would be the sacrifice of Christ upon the cross and the idea that he "died for our sins".

In Hebrew the word for Life, *chai* (חי), has a value of 18 (10+8), which is the ordinal value of Tzaddik, as the eighteenth letter. Its gematria value of 90 ties back into the word *manna* (מן) whose value is also 90 and relates directly to the idea of *receiving one's life-sustenance*. Recall that the word Tree in Hebrew, *otz* (עץ), is composed of the letters Ayin (ע : eye) and Tzaddik (צ : humble servant), suggesting that the visionary power of a tzaddik reveals the **Tree of Life.**

During the original creative act, God says "Let us make man in our image" (Genesis 1:26) and the word **image** in Hebrew is *tselem* (צלם). According to the Jewish faith, our life is sustained by the grace of God who has created us in his image. Thus the righteous one, the tzaddik, must surrender to their role as an *image of God*, and in doing so will merge with God and become an embodied reflection of God. In the book of Proverbs (10:25) we read "As the whirlwind passeth, so the wicked one is no more, but the righteous one (*tzaddik*) is an everlasting foundation (*yesod olam*)." Bearing in mind that Yesod, the ninth sphere of life, relates to the sacral-sexual chakra of the human body, the implication of this quote has to do with purification of our sexual energies through prayer and service to God.

When the kundalini energy of Yesod is directed upward toward Kether, like the Yod-hand of Tzaddik that reaches up to God, we restore life-force energy (*chai*) to the Tree (*otz*) and our consciousness returns to its original place in Upper Eden. The fountain of eternal youth pours down from Kether in return. This is the sexual meaning of Tzaddik. In a similar way, when we extend compassion to others and sacrifice our selfish desires for sensual pleasure, our soul-energy is conserved and raised up to the level of the heart, which circulates through the body and fills us with light. At the deepest layer of reality, i.e. the subatomic quantum field, there is no physicality or materiality. Everything is made up of photons of light, including our body and consciousness, so that we are literally "images" in the imagination of God. To cultivate our light-body is to embody more of reality. In Hebrew the word *tzadekah* means charity, connecting to the idea of *tzimtzum* in that, when we receive this light, the compassionate thing to do is to give it away. There is no shortage of light because everything is made of light. In true charity, nothing is lost.

The Personal Subconscious

Qoph

ק

Tone-Color:	B – Violet-Red
Letter Symbolism:	Back of the Head
Tarot Card:	The Moon
Gematria Value:	100
Astrology:	Pisces
Tree of Life Path:	Path 29 from Netzach to Malkuth

Qabalistic Significance

The shape of the letter **Qoph** may be interpreted as the combination of Vav and Kaph, the disjunction between the two emphasizing a distinction between spinal column and skull. The *Sepher Yetzirah* attributes Qoph to the cerebellum, which it calls corporeal intelligence, the primitive part of our brain responsible for basic motor skills and movement-related coordination. On the tree of life, Qoph bridges Netzach, the sphere of Venus, to Malkuth, the sphere of Earth, taking the path-worker down into the material world. Its tarot card is The Moon, suggesting that on this path the divine light cannot be seen directly. The meaning of the letter is "back of the head" which relates to all of the aforementioned symbolism, including the shape of Kaph as a head, the location of the cerebellum, and the invisibility of light (unless you have eyes in the back of your head). The other common meaning of Qoph (קוֹפ) in Hebrew is "ape", which could represent a less evolved form of human being but may also relate to the Egyptian ape-headed *God of the Mind*, **Thoth**.

If you recall, Gimel means "thick rope" and symbolizes the spine reaching down from the back of the head to its foundation in Yesod. In its correspondence to the Moon card, Qoph resonates with the High Priestess, whose planetary attribution is the moon. The biblical passage about Gimel passing through the eye of a needle is relevant here, as Qoph in Aramaic means "eye of a needle". As our number one blind spot, the back of the head corresponds to the *personal subconscious*. In the simplest terms, it represents what we literally cannot see with our eyes, but to be more accurate it has to do with the aspects of our psyche that exist and persist without our awareness. Included in this would be the world of dreams, instincts, unconscious biases and beliefs.

Each sphere on the Tree of Life has a planetary attribution. The moon is attributed to the **ninth sphere**, Yesod. As the 18th key of the tarot, Qoph mirrors the value of Yesod by doubling it (9x2=18). The gematria value of Yesod (יסוד: 4+6+60+10=80) has been linked by Kabbalists to Qoph via the word life, Chai (חי =8+10=18) through multiplication (8x10=80=Yesod).

Yesod has been called Lower Eden or Eve, in contrast to Upper Eden, Adam, which is attributed to the crowning sphere of Kether. Qoph's ordinal value as the 19th letter of the Hebrew Alphabet correlates to the biblical spelling of Eve as *Chavah* (חוה: 5+6+8=19). Though the position of Yesod/Eve/Lower Eden appears to be subordinate to its opposite pole in Kether, it plays an equally important role in the Tree. Without Yesod there could be no embodiment of Spirit. At the same time, in its close relationship to our animal nature, Qoph and Yesod teach the importance of taming our instincts so as to preserve the divine spark of light within.

When the sexual energy of Yesod is misdirected and ejaculated from the body, the light of the Tree of Life vanishes and its spheres become Qlippoth (קליפות) translating to English as "Empty Shells". Then the moon is denied its designated role as a reflective surface for the radiance of the sun. Malkuth, the lowest sphere on the tree, becomes endarkened. This is the nature of the ape, *Qoph*, who spills its seed carelessly and therefore can never develop its intellect.

Solar Radiance

Resh

Tone-Color:	D – Orange
Letter Symbolism:	Face
Tarot Card:	The Sun
Gematria Value:	200
Astrology:	Sol
Tree of Life Path:	Path 30 from Hod to Yesod

Qabalistic Significance

Rotating 180 degrees to the other side of the head, we move sequentially from Qoph to **Resh**, which in Hebrew means "face" and corresponds to human consciousness and ego-identity. It features a strong solar element, not only in its astrological and tarot attributions, but also in its use throughout the Hebrew lexicon. A number of words indicating traditional "solar" qualities begin with Resh, such as the word for beginnings, *resheit* (ראשית) and the word *rabah* (רבה) meaning to multiply and increase. The word Resh (ראש) is composed of a Resh and the word *ash* (אש) that in Hebrew means **fire**, suggesting the "fire of the head". This creative fire is invoked in the very first word of genesis, *beresheit*, and is implied in the title *roshi*, an acronym for *Rabbi Shlomo Itzhaki*, a major rabbinical figure during the 11th century revered for his profound and simple interpretations of the Talmud, the meditations upon Torah. Intellectual strength that can be enjoyed and understood by all is a function of a healthy Resh. The figure of Christ, as the son/sun of God, is equally relevant here.

Both the Crown of the Tree of Life, *Keter* (כתר), and the cocoon of light that envelops it, *Ain Soph Aur* (אין סוף אור), end in the letter Resh, signifying their mutual radiance. The word *aur*, meaning light, is composed of an Aleph, Vav and Resh. As we know by now, Aleph relates to the Breath of Spirit and Vav relates to the Spine, therefore the light signified by the word *Aur* refers not just to visible light, but to the *energy* that rises up the spine and into the head through breath to form a **halo of light** around the Resh (head/face).

In Hebrew the word *ruach* (רוח) means "spirit" and "wind" and is closely related to the Imagination. When the shape of Resh is laid over a left-facing profile of the human head, it aligns so that its upper Yod touches the forehead and the column of Resh reaches back and down toward the base of the head (Qoph). Whatever we perceive consciously is processed and embellished by the creative imagination, channeled through the reflective nature of Qoph, down the spine, to Yesod, and touches the foundation of our Being. Therefore, the thoughts cultivated in our head have a direct influence on our emotions and instinctual reactions.

Depending on what we feed our head, our actions may manifest as ethical or not. The word *rasha* (רשע) appears in the Book of Isaiah 48:22 when God states that there is no rest for the *wicked*. The word *rash* (ראש) means "poverty" and suggests a lack of moral values, and *ra* means "evil" as in the expression *lashon ha-ra* (לשון הרע) which refers to the proverbial "evil tongue" and *ayin hara*, the "evil eye". In both instances, it relates to the derogatory speech or attitudes towards another. To gossip is to commit *rechilut* (רכילות), a sin according to a line in Leviticus (19:6).

In contrast, the word *rav* (רב) means "great" and is the root of the word "rabbi" (רבי), compelling us not to make generalizations about the inherent meaning of a single letter. Resh is neither implicitly wicked nor is it great. When we are in balance and cultivating compassion, signified in Hebrew by the word *racham* (רחם), the thoughts in our head will lead us to virtuous actions, leading us to *Raziel* (רזיאל), the "Angel of Mysteries" in Jewish mysticism.

Creator, Sustainer, and Destroyer

Shin

Tone-Color:	C – Red
Letter Symbolism:	Tooth
Tarot Card:	Judgment
Gematria Value:	300
Astrology:	Pluto
Tree of Life Path:	Path 31 from Hod to Malkuth

Qabalistic Significance

Shape informs the inner meaning of all 22 Hebrew letters, but few are so explicitly symbolic as the letter Shin. Its gematria value is 300 (3+0+0=3) and its ordinal value as the 21st letter (2+1=3) reduces to the same amount. Its three crowning Yods represent the idea of **trinity** under the guise of the letters Vav, Zayin, and Nun (ו, ז, נ). As the second letter of *ash* (שׁא) it connects to the idea of fire, and because Yod has been compared to both "God's finger" and a "candle flame", the trinity of extensions from Shin's base loosely correlate to candle sticks. If the three pillars were candles, these yods would illuminate the supernal triad of *Binah, Kether, and Chokmah.* Of the four Kabbalistic Worlds, Shin implicates *Atziluth, Briah and Yetzirah,* the archetypal, creative, and formative planes of Being. It simultaneously connects to the Kabbalistic concept of the three Mother Letters, Aleph, Mem, and Shin (שׁמא), which unfold at the center of the Kabbalistic rose and represent the elements of Air, Water and Fire, or in human terms, the domains of **intellect, emotion, and instinct.**

One of the early Judaic names of God, by which Abraham knew Him, was *Al Shadai* (אל שדי), meaning "Lord Almighty". In Exodus 6:2-3, the true name of God as tetragrammaton (יהוה) is revealed to Moses but not to Abraham, Isaac or Jacob. The spelling of the name Shadai implies trinity (Shin) transitioning (Daleth/Door) to unity (Yod) and etymologically connects to the word *shadad* (שדד), which means "destroyer" or "strength". Interestingly, the Hindu deity Shiva is also called the "destroyer of worlds" and begins with the same consonant sound of *sh*. He is commonly shown holding a **trident**, the three-pronged fork that Westerners would typically associate with the Greek God Neptune. Shiva belongs to the Hindu *trimurti*, or trinity of gods, the other two being Brahma (the creator) and Vishnu (the sustainer), bringing us back to the threefold nature of the letter **Shin**.

The B.O.T.A tarot deck correlates the Hebrew letter Peh (**mouth**) to the Tower card, an image representing God's destructive power. Consider this in relation to the Hebrew word *shin* (שין) that means "tooth", something that dwells in the mouth and whose purpose is as a *destroyer* or *transformer* of food. Closely related to Shin are the words *shinoy* (שינוי) meaning "change" and *shana* (שנה) meaning "year". This brings us to another tarot card, the Wheel of Fortune, which represents **cycles of change** and features another trinity of god-forms. Rising up counterclockwise is Anubis, protector-god ruling over the dead, in contrast to the descending image of Typhon, the most evil "monster of monsters". Crowning the wheel is a sphinx, a benevolent but ferocious guardian of the Mysteries.

The ten spheres of the tree of life divide into the supernal triad and the seven lower spheres. In this way, Malkuth may be interpreted as either the tenth or seventh sphere. When viewed as the latter, it connects to the Jewish day of rest, Shabbat (שבת), the seventh and final day of the week, reserved for rest and spiritual contemplation. Rabbi Isaac Luria of the 16th century wrote a famous hymn about Shabbat, describing it as a queen and bride, and in the Talmud there are many allusions to the Shabbat's feminine attributes, correlating it to the Shekinah (שכניה), the feminine aspect of God.

Completion and Prayer

Tav

Tone-Color:	A – Blue-Violet
Letter Symbolism:	Seal/Stamp
Tarot Card:	The World
Gematria Value:	400
Astrology:	Saturn
Tree of Life Path:	Path 32 from Yesod to Malkuth

Qabalistic Significance

Tav is positioned at the center of the Qabalistic cube and represents the completion of our journey through the Hebrew alphabet, like the waxen seal upon the back of an envelope or a signature at the end of a document. It is the final letter of the Hebrew word *emet* (אמת), which means "truth", as well as the first and last letter of Tiphareth (תפארת), the sixth sphere and radiant soul-center of the Tree of Life. Corresponding to this sixth sphere is the sixth letter, Vav ו, whose inner meaning implies both the spine and phallus. Tav is spelled תו and on the tree of life is the path that connects Yesod to Malkuth, representing the base of the spine and root chakra. As the 22nd letter (2+2=4) it relates closely to the cross with Christ at its center, evidenced by its corresponding tarot card, The World, whose imagery shows the fully revealed and divine androgyne positioned between the four fixed astrological signs. Actually, the ancient Phoenician letter tau was a cross (X) much like the English letter "t", marking the intersection between vertical and horizontal planes.

All of Judaism rests on the teachings and laws of the Torah (תורה),
of which the first two letters spell the word Tav (תו). The word Tav
is also contained in the word Talmud (תלמוד), the other three
letters LMD spelling out the Hebrew letter Lamed (ל). The Talmud
contains the teachings and perspectives of thousands of rabbis over
the course of many centuries. Lamed corresponds to the tarot card
Justice, whose imagery features a character bearing a sword in one
hand and scales in the other, alluding to the Egyptian figure Ma'at, a
goddess of justice who weighs the souls of the dead to determine
whether they are fit to enter the kingdom of Heaven. In Hebrew, the
same word m'at (מאת) appears where Mem is an article meaning
"of" and Aleph-Tav signifies something equivalent to the Greek
Alpha-Omega, as if alluding to the intermediary realm between
death and life, the very place that one would expect to encounter the
Egyptian Ma'at.

The final verse of the Song of Solomon includes the idea of Tav as a
seal, reciting "Set me as **a seal** upon thine heart, as a **seal** upon thine
arm: for love is strong as death", evoking again the imagery of Christ
and the cross, albeit prior to his arrival on Earth. Christ's murder
upon the cross alludes to the letter Tav, marking the completion of
the prophecy that a messiah would come to redeem the Jewish
people. His name in Hebrew, Yeheshuah (יהשוה), introduced a
fifth letter, Shin, to the tetragrammaton, signifying a radiant point of
light at the center of the four lettered name of god. As the
pentagrammaton, his name invokes the law of Man in relation to
God, the sacred heart at the center of left-right-above-below.

Prayer and repentance are known in Hebrew as *teshuvah* (תשובה)
which literally means "return" and is considered to be the way of
atoning for sinful behavior during this incarnation. When we face
Ma'at in the gates between worlds, the lightness or heaviness of our
heart will be a function of how much self-work we have done.
According to the Talmud, God created teshuvah prior to creating the
physical universe. This hints at balance as the True Nature of the
human soul. Life in the World constantly tempts us to sin. Insofar as
we have given in to these temptations, the rabbis teach that we
should pray in this life to liberate our soul from its karmic debts.

RECAPITULATION OF THE 22 LETTERS

1)   א Aleph: Sacred Breath

2)   ב Beth: House of God

3)   ג Gimel: Holy Spirit

4)   ד Daleth: The Door

5)   ה Heh: Thought Speech and Action

6)   ו Vav: Spinal Column

7)   ז Zayin: Double-Edged Tongue

8)   ח Cheth: The Inner Self

9)   ט Teth: Kundalini and Sexual Energy

10)   י Yod: Universal Flame of Consciousness

20)   כ Kaph: The Golden Cap

30)   ל Lamed: Heart of the Mind

40)   מ Mem: Creative Waters

50)   נ Nun: Sperm and Body

60)   ס Samekh: Unlimited Serpent Power

70)   ע Ayin: Consciousness in the World

80)   פ Peh: Chaos, Destruction, and the Mood of Apocalypse

90)   צ Tzaddik: Compassion as Sustenance

100)   ק Qoph: Personal Subconscious

200)   ר Resh: The Head and Face of God

300)   ש Shin: Creator, Sustainer, and Destroyer

400)   ת Tav: Completion and Prayer

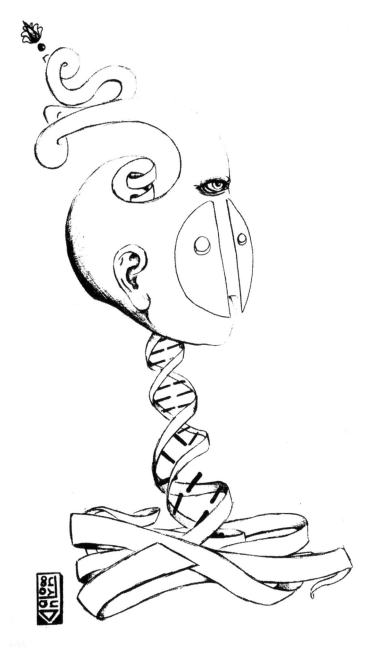

Tracing the Breadcrumbs Back to Source-Consciousness

Cosmogenic DNA: The Tree in the Seed

We are planetary entities. Our journey around the sun seems to be informed by a harmonic relationship to the other planets in our solar system, the harmony of the spheres, onto which astrologers have projected various aspects of their psychological makeup for eons. Enveloping this solar system is our galactic home, the Milky Way, composed of many stellar constellations. Western astrologers divide this galactic disk into twelve parts, which we call zodiac signs, onto which we overlay further layers of mythic and archetypal content. From the anthropocentric perspective, human beings are the bridge between Heaven and Earth. Whatever we discover *outside* is mirrored *within*.

Human consciousness orients itself toward the material world in a number of ways, primarily in terms of spatial location. We have developed sophisticated methods of measuring our position in space by observing changes in our physical environment along the one-dimensional track of chronological time. The most fundamental observations of space-time happen through the immediacy of human perception, which can be modeled as a point positioned at the center of a cube looking outward to the six faces as directional reference points. As we move through chronological time, the appearance of sensory input from the six directions of the cube continually shifts.

3-D Euclidean space and chronological time may seem like adequate models for describing the Western mode of human perception. But they present some problems when we inquire into the nature of consciousness itself. The center of the Cube represents the center of **perception** and behaves like a **black hole**. If we attribute creative potency to perception, then the center of the cube appears as both a **black and white hole**. Either way, this center functions as a zero-dimensional singularity. The idea that black holes lead somewhere, like a wormhole or *Einstein-Rosen bridge*, brings up the inevitable question regarding **what kind of space** awaits us on the other side.

So far, I have proposed that metaphorically, this zero-dimensional point could lead to a 4+ dimensional reality. Our ancestors made a valiant effort to philosophically and even theologically bridge the gap between human life and mundane perceptions into the boundless mystery of deep inner space.

Forging a devotional relationship to their imagined sense of God, early psychonauts like the Kabbalists channeled and explored their treasured religious texts, turning them around every which way and contemplating the intratextual meanings at every level, as if it were composed in a fractal structure.

Unlike the English language, which we tend to take at face value as a transactional and dialogical means of communication, Kabbalistic texts unveiled a wealth of spiritual and practical meanings in the Torah that were attributed to the shape and numerical values of the letters themselves, along with the words forged from them. A well-known Kabbalistic text called the *Sepher Yetzirah* refers to the **231 gates** (22x21), composed of every possible two-letter combination, each with its own unique meaning. Every word had a semantic role that was greater than the sum of its parts, and yet was simultaneously informed by the *gates*, which is to say that each two-letter combination within a word had its own unique meaning that contributed to the meaning of the 3+letter word-aggregates.

In attributing the twenty-two letters of the Hebrew alphabet to the 22 aspects of the cube of space, archetypal patterns emerged between the letter-meanings and their spatial orientation in the cube itself, which resonate in turn with the twenty-two paths on the Tree of Life. As a 2-d representation of our 3-d physical orientation in space, the cube demonstrates in clear terms how a 3+Dimensional object can be flattened into a two-dimensional representation on paper.

Now that we have explored in detail the meaning of the Hebrew letters as they map onto the cube, as well as the 4+D **Tree of Life**, we are going to trace the 2-d design of the Tree back to an even more fundamental geometric design called the Seed of Life, which according to many historians is in fact where the Tree's shape was originally derived. All of the attributions to the Hebrew letters, including their tarot, planetary, and tone color correspondences, will be temporarily left behind as we dissolve into the harmony of the Seed's perfect circles.

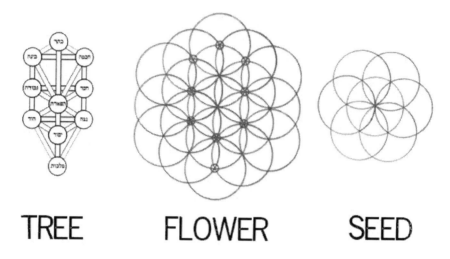

TREE   FLOWER   SEED

The Tree of Life is made up of ten spheres and twenty-two paths that connect them, excluding for now the hidden 11th sphere, Da'ath. To draw the spheres in correct proportion to one another, a grid must be established. These days, we tend to think of a grid as the waffle-shaped Cartesian Coordinates (X and Y axes). Even circular graphing formats like military radar systems overlay square grids upon the concentric circles to help orient the operator. We are a culture of squares and boxes.

The Flower of Life represents an alternative - a circular grid out of which the square-shaped grid can be derived. The Tree of Life on the left demonstrates this clearly; the three horizontal paths (*Hod* to *Netzach, Chesed* to *Geburah*, and *Binah* to *Chokmah)* intersect with the three vertical pillars of the Tree to create a 2x2 grid of four equal quadrants. This shape is the root geometry of Cartesian coordinates. In the second, middle image shown above, I have illustrated how the spheres of the Tree are derived from the **Flower of Life**. Each sphere on the tree signifies the perfectly symmetrical intersection of three circles. The **Flower of Life** is a secondary, algorithmic iteration of a previous shape called the **Seed of Life**. It would be accurate to say that the Tree comes from the Flower, which comes from the Seed. Where then does the Seed of Life come from?

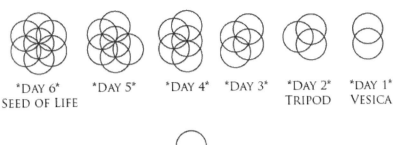

DAY 6   *DAY 5*   *DAY 4*   *DAY 3*   *DAY 2*   *DAY 1*
SEED OF LIFE   TRIPOD   VESICA

UNITY

*"And God said, "Let there be light," and there was light. God saw that the light was good, and he separated the light from the darkness. God called the light "day," and the darkness he called "night." And there was evening, and there was morning—**the first day**."*

*"And God said, "Let there be a vault between the waters to separate water from water." So God made the vault and separated the water under the vault from the water above it. And it was so. God called the vault "sky." And there was evening, and there was morning—**the second day**."*

"And God said, "Let the water under the sky be gathered to one place, and let dry ground appear." And it was so. [10] *God called the dry ground "land," and the gathered waters he called "seas." And God saw that it was good...*

*"Then God said, "Let the land produce vegetation: seed-bearing plants and trees on the land that bear fruit with seed in it, according to their various kinds." And it was so. The land produced vegetation: plants bearing seed according to their kinds and trees bearing fruit with seed in it according to their kinds. And God saw that it was good. And there was evening, and there was morning—**the third day**."*

"And God said, "Let there be lights in the vault of the sky to separate the day from the night, and let them serve as signs to mark sacred times, and days and years, and let them be lights in the vault of the sky to give light on the earth." And it was so. God made two great lights—the greater light to govern the day and the lesser light to govern the night. He also made the stars. God set

them in the vault of the sky to give light on the earth, to govern the day and the night, and to separate light from darkness. And God saw that it was good. And there was evening, and there was morning—**the fourth day**."

"And God said, "Let the water teem with living creatures, and let birds fly above the earth across the vault of the sky." So God created the great creatures of the sea and every living thing with which the water teems and that moves about in it, according to their kinds, and every winged bird according to its kind. And God saw that it was good. God blessed them and said, "Be fruitful and increase in number and fill the water in the seas, and let the birds increase on the earth." And there was evening, and there was morning—**the fifth day**."

"And God said, "Let the land produce living creatures according to their kinds: the livestock, the creatures that move along the ground, and the wild animals, each according to its kind." And it was so. [25] God made the wild animals according to their kinds, the livestock according to their kinds, and all the creatures that move along the ground according to their kinds. And God saw that it was good.

"Then God said, "Let us make mankind in our image, in our likeness, so that they may rule over the fish in the sea and the birds in the sky, over the livestock and all the wild animals, and over all the creatures that move along the ground."

"So God created mankind in his own image, in the image of God he created them; male and female he created them. God blessed them and said to them, "Be fruitful and increase in number; fill the earth and subdue it. Rule over the fish in the sea and the birds in the sky and over every living creature that moves on the ground."

"Then God said, "I give you every seed-bearing plant on the face of the whole earth and every tree that has fruit with seed in it. They will be yours for food. And to all the beasts of the earth and all the birds in the sky and all the creatures that move along the ground—everything that has the breath of life in it—I give every green plant for food." And it was so. God saw all that he had made, and it was very good. And there was evening, and there was morning—**the sixth day.**

Sacred Geometric Genesis and the Seed of Life

*"Thus the heavens and the earth were completed in all their vast array. By the seventh day God had finished the work he had been doing; so on the seventh day he rested from all his work. Then God blessed **the seventh day** and made it holy, because on it he rested from all the work of creating that he had done."*

The Seed of Life has been interpreted by both sacred geometers and kabbalists to be a two-dimensional symbolic representation of the hypothetical **4+Dimensional Creative Process** described in the biblical book of Genesis (1:3-2:3). When we reverse engineer the story, beginning with the seventh day and moving back to Original Unity, it becomes clear how the **origin of the Seed** is a **Circle** with a point at its center. This Circle is simply a **2-d cross-section of a Sphere**, which could be geometrically interpreted as a three-dimensional cross-section of a **4+dimensional Hyper-Sphere** (i.e. the original and upper-dimensional form of **God**).

The first day of creation is described in Genesis as the separation of Light from Dark. In the illustration below, I have represented this symbolically and coined a new term for the Vesica Pisces, calling the two interlocking circles "Circumferential Centers". Any given point along the circumference of an original circle can become the center-point of a new circle, and vice versa, the center of that first circle will become part of the circumferential continuum of the second circle. When we trace the Seed of Life back from the seventh day to the second day, we get the circumferential centers, and when we trace the second day back to the first, we arrive at Kether, the crown of the Tree of Life and Creative Center of the Seed of Life.

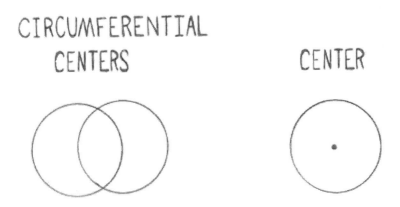

CIRCUMFERENTIAL CENTERS   CENTER

The Proverbial Chicken and the Egg

As a young person I couldn't help but wonder about the origins of God. It made sense to me that there *could be* a higher order of reality in which a creator-figure was orchestrating the events of life on Earth. What irked me about this idea was the riddle of the chicken and the egg. If God created the universe, who or what created God?

When I asked people for their opinion about this, the same few answers always pinged back. Some folks shrugged and told me they didn't know. Some got triggered and told me to *just have faith*. But the more mystically inclined characters, with a sparkle in their eye, suggested that God was Eternal and existed outside the boundaries of space and time. I always felt that the last answer was closest to the truth, but I couldn't wrap my head around what this really meant.

In discovering the Kabbalistic Tree, the logic of cosmogenesis began to make sense to me. The first and uppermost sphere, Kether, was described as a point at the center of a circle from which the whole Tree shot forth like a bolt of lightning. Kether was itself an emergent function of what Kabbalists call the *tzimtzum*, **a phase** of **contraction** from *Ain Soph Aur*, which in Hebrew means **Limitless Light. Ain Soph Aur** is represented as three concentric spheres around Kether, progressing from Ain (**Nothing**) to Ain Soph (**Limitlessness**) to Ain Soph Aur (**Limitless Light**). A.S.A.'s original condition is Eternity.

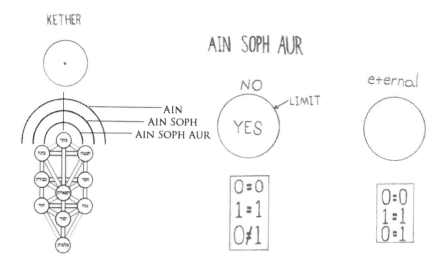

AIN SOPH AUR

"Form is Emptiness - Emptiness is form - Form is none other than Emptiness - Emptiness is none other than Form" – Heart Sutra

"Before He gave any shape to the world, before He produced any form, He was alone, without form and without resemblance to anything else" – The Zohar

"In itself, it is unknowable, unthinkable, and unspeakable" – Israel Regardie

"Music is the space between the notes" – Claude Debussy

"Space is the Place" – Sun Ra

KETHER

"The diamond is attributed to Kether, because it is the most permanent and glittering of precious jewels." – Israel Regardie

"Everything has a point, and if it doesn't, there's no point to It." – Harry Nilsson

The original *voice of God* had no-thing to talk about. Its individuality was achieved by way of a contraction from the boundlessness of its True Nature as Limitless Light. Collapsing into a zero-dimensional point, what Kabbalists call **Kether,** this point at the center of *Ain Soph Aur* could only define itself according to the circumference. There could be no implicit meaning in the creative word of God other than Ain Soph Aur because nothing else existed. Thus the emergence of One from the womb-tomb of Zero marks the beginning and end of all known forms. The upper-dimensional template of the physical-material universe as we know it, represented symbolically by the Tree of Life, traces its multiplicity of forms back to the original condition in Eternity, yet even the idea of "tracing back" is meaningless. ***Eternity is an omnipresent situation.***

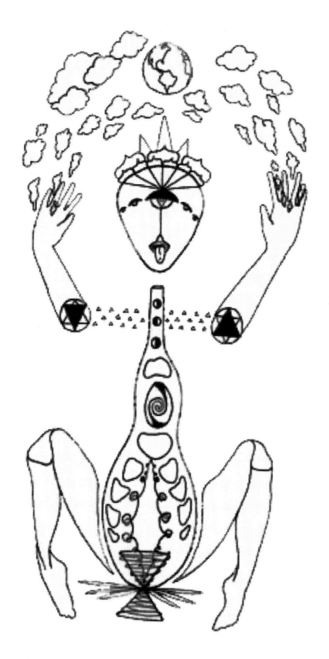

From Source-Consciousness to the Whole of Creation

Fall From Eden: The Original Sine Wave

ACOUSTIC TONES

"Tao produced Unity, Unity produced Duality, Duality produced Trinity, and Trinity produced all existing things" – Lao Tsu

"Geometry is frozen Music" - Goethe

Our most common ideas about sound and music are based on percussion waves and the relatively dense perceptual faculties of the ear. Yet according to the Greek philosopher Pythagoras, and countless others, there exists a more pure music than the physical sounds of this world. Such music can be perceived in trance states and in dreams as an intense, profound sensation presented to our consciousness by some mysterious agency. Let's imagine that the origin of this divine inner music was none other than the creative word of God extending its influence from the multidimensional, nonlocal field of *Ain Soph Aur*, through Kether, all the way down the Tree of Life and straight into our soul. Cultivating a direct relationship with this phenomenon, called the *harmony of the spheres* by the Greeks, we overcome our dependency upon the concepts of religious ideology and develop a real-time interface with Source-Consciousness... a kind of **Musical Gnosis**.

We have established how the Kabbalistic **Tree of Life** traces geometric roots back to the **Seed of Life, Kether**, and the Empty Fullness of **Eternity** (0=1). The next phase of our work is to demonstrate how this progression of sacred symbols relates graphically to the biblical idea of an Original Word, and in turn, how this original word corresponds to the idea of music. I would like to demonstrate now how music, typically defined as either **notes** (forms existing in the mind) or **tones** (perceptions of physical vibrations), owes its existence to an Original Tone. Without an original tone there could be no human perception of tone, and without perception of a tone there could be no arrangement of sound waves into the harmonically agreeable melodies and chord progressions that we call Music.

Kether as Original Word: Unit Circles and the Sine Wave

Kabbalistic texts describe the origin of Kether as an omnidirectional contraction from *Ain Soph Aur*, the *empty-fullness of the Universe*, into a zero-point at the center of its own limitless light. The Hebrew letter Yod ׳, whose inner meanings are "finger of god" and "candle flame", has been attributed to Kether because the center of a circle is singular, like a pointing finger. Since God is not actually an old bearded man in the sky, he/she/it has no meat-body or physical finger to speak of, so the symbol of a small flame somehow seems more appropriate.

Of course, it goes without saying that the poetry of kabbalah is not intended to be taken literally. Nobody stares at a blank canvass and cause its empty surface to spontaneously contract into a dot at the center of a circle. So, if we wish to acquire a 2-dimensional representation of Kether on paper, we have to go about this creative act by alternate means. The most obvious way to draw a perfect circle is with a compass, adjusting the hinge so that it stays fixed at one angle, anchoring the pointed spike onto the page and rotating the pen or pencil 360 degrees around that center point.

Many esoteric teachings have interpreted this creative geometric act philosophically. The fraternal order of Freemasonry draws upon the iconic **square and compass** for their logo. It was described by high-ranking freemason Albert Pike, author of *Morals and Dogma*, in the following way:

> *"**The compass** is an instrument that has relation to spheres and spherical surfaces, and is adapted to spherical trigonometry, or that branch of mathematics which **deals with the Heavens and the orbits of the planetary bodies.**"* [14]

Our ancestors developed a highly sophisticated understanding of astronomy based on circular measurements of the celestial spheres. These early astronomers and natural philosophers held that planetary orbits followed perfect circular trajectories around the Earth. Whether or not they literally believed that the orbits were circular, or had simply chosen the circle as an elegant metaphor, we can say with certainty that circles have always been exploited to represent the celestial macrocosm. **Kabbalistic thought has represented the original word of God with a circle, as described in the following pages.**

---

[14] Morals and Dogma: Consistory: XXXII. Sublime of the Royal Secret pg. 850-51

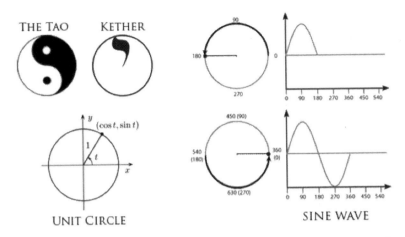

THE TAO   KETHER

UNIT CIRCLE   SINE WAVE

Circles have long served as icons for both the physical heavens as well as the higher-dimensional heavens described by mystical texts like the biblical book of Genesis. To draw **Kether,** the crown of the Tree of Life represented by a point at the center of a circle, we need a compass and a piece of paper. In the image above you can see how the base of the Hebrew letter Yod ＇ connects to the center of a circle, and how, like a compass, the Yod shape rotates 360 degrees around this center to create the circle's circumference. Trigonometry, a branch of mathematics that studies the relationship between triangles and circles, illustrates how **the creation of a Unit Circle simultaneously generates a shape called the Sine Wave.**

How does the circle create a sine wave, you ask? In simple terms, the X-Axis of the Sine Wave graph is defined by progress along the circumference of a circle. One full sine wave has a wavelength of 360 degrees, a direct result of the full 360-degree rotation along the circle's circumference. If you were to snip the circle at its starting point and uncoil it so that it was laid out in a straight line, you would have the x-axis of the Sine Wave graph. The Y-Axis values of the circle and sine wave are identical. When the y-value of the circle goes up or down, so does the sine wave. In mathematics, **sine waves** are defined as a smooth and repetitious oscillation between opposite poles. They are composed of a single frequency without any harmonic overtones, meaning that they are "pure" tones similar to the sound produced by a vibrating tuning fork.

As established in the previous chapter, the seven days of creation can be symbolically represented by a series of circles that generate the Seed of Life. Each of these creative days was the result of God's speech, and what is speech if not a meaningful sound wave? Co-arising with the creation of a circle, the sine wave seems to me to be a perfect metaphor for the original creative word of God. The attribution of tone-frequency to the circle imbues the flower of life with a musical quality and has major implications with regards to the Harmony of the Spheres.

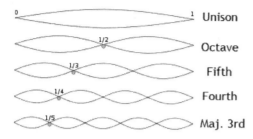

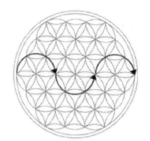

Musical Intervals as Sine Waves

Example: The "Fifth" Interval
On the Flower of Life

So far we know that the unit circle produces a sine wave, and that acoustical physics refers to sine waves as a tool for graphic measurement of single tone-frequencies. In the image above you can see on the left how whole number ratios (1:1, 1:2, 2:3, 3:4, 4:5, etc.) between individual tones produces the familiar musical intervals of the octave, perfect fifth, perfect fourth, and major third. On the right side is an image of the Flower of Life with a sine wave projected out upon its surface, illustrating how the spheres of the Flower can describe sine waves and musical intervals.

Prior to Kepler's discovery of the elliptical orbit, our astronomical models described planetary orbits as nested spheres surrounding earth, represented 2-dimensionally by concentric circles. Egyptian, Jewish and Greek metaphysics drew upon the flower of life as an emblem of their astronomical models. Seeking to describe the root-origin of the heavenly macrocosm, astronomers conjured a creation story in texts like the opening chapter of Genesis that would eloquently summarize their belief system. A major part of this story, evidenced by their emphasis upon creative speech and the "Harmony of the Spheres", was sound-frequency and music. Each planet, spinning through space along fixed periodic cycles of orbit, created its own unique musical tone. The highness and lowness of a planet's musical pitch was determined by the speed of its orbit around the earth. Even today, we could apply this same logic to the orbit of planets around the sun. It makes sense intuitively, even if we do not yet have the scientific means of measuring these planetary tones.

Sound Waves and the Cymatic Mandalas of 4-D Reality

In the previous chapter I laid out the basic geometric premise of God's original word, representing it as a unit-circle and sine wave frequency. The implication here is that God's word, as a musical tone, introduced structure to the cosmic soup of proto-stardust, i.e. the condition prior to what scientists call the Big Bang, sculpting and giving shape to everything in the known macrocosmic and microscopic worlds of physical 4-D reality. From this perspective, the planets not only generate tones through their periodic movement through space; they would literally be molded and held together by those tones, as if there were a musical template of harmonic proportions underlying all of reality. This was the belief held by our ancient ancestors and is nicely illustrated in Robert Fludd's 17th century depiction of the *Celestial Monochord*. What evidence do we have in our physical world today that individual sound frequencies can organize matter into geometric forms?

All the world's great Mystery traditions have sought ways to physically represent the influence of sound upon material structures. Simultaneous with the Greek Pythagorean and Platonic schools of philosophy during the 4th -6th century B.C., the Taoist mystics of China were experimenting with what has been translated to English as "jumping water basins" or "spouting bowls". The design of these bowls is relatively simple, usually made from a bronze alloy and shaped something like a frying pan, with small handles on opposite sides of the bowl. The practitioner pours water into the bowl, and with the palms of their hands, rubs the handles back and forth to create a sound frequency that vibrates through the water to produce what in physics would be called a *standing wave,* or stationary geometric waveform pattern. This happens because the friction between one's hands and the bowl's handles sends the basin into vibratory resonance. Like dropping a rock into water as a way of generating concentric waves, we can pump a musical tone through water and generate not only concentric circles, but a variety of other geometries as well.

When a sound wave frequency is held constant and vibrated through a surface membrane, usually a metal plate topped with an excitatory medium like water, sand, or cornstarch, it can produce fascinating geometric forms. The study of this method belongs to the scientific field of *cymatics*. From the Greek word cyma, meaning wave, these cymatic forms are *modal phenomena* arising from resonant standing wave patterns, or fields, produced by the sound wave. They tend to resemble the circular symmetry of a mandala. Cymatics offers strong evidence that sound has a formative influence upon the organization of physical structures. If you have never heard of or seen cymatic imagery before, I recommend scouring the Internet for some video footage. The term cymatics was coined by Swiss natural scientist Hans Jenny in his 1967 book *Kymatic (volume 1)*, though the Western world was introduced to these methods centuries prior with the work of 18th century German physicist Ernst Chladni. His research demonstrated how geometric figures could be produced by drawing a violin bow upon the edge of a metal plate topped with sand.

The observations and insights derived from experimental work with cymatics can be applied to many other areas of natural science. The surface of our planet, when struck by lightning, produces a deep humming sound and standing wave form whose frequency undergoes continuous oscillations in the resonant cavity *between heaven and earth*. Predicted first by Winfried Otto Schumann in the early 1950's and later proven accurate by a pair of scientists in the early 1960's, the *Schumann resonance* was identified as a phenomena arising from the *closed waveguide* between the surface of our planet and our conductive ionosphere. Imagine a sine wave where the amplitude (height) of the wave is determined by the space between Earth and its upper atmosphere, forming a resonant cavity encircling the earth that holds space for the propagation of electromagnetic waves in the *extremely low frequency* band. Note the similarity to earlier descriptions in this book about how unit circles produce sine waves, correlating to Earth and the Schumann frequency.

When lightning strikes, jolts of electrical current send the *electro magnetic field* of our planet into motion, resulting in a standing wave pattern whose wavelength is equal to the circumference of earth. There is plentiful evidence that similar resonant fields exist on the other planets of our solar system. The scientific model of resonance presented by Schumann is hardly fifty years old, but its central proposition is an ancient one. In his essay on *Acoustic Symbolism*, musicologist Marius Schneider cites the fourth Veda of Hindu Scripture, the *Atharva Veda,* to depict a symbol of the Creator's mouth, whose "upper jaw was the sky and lower jaw was the earth". Here we find a key to understanding the relationship between cosmology and modern science, where the image of the creator's mouth as a hollow cave is superimposed upon Earth's resonant cavity, the space between ground and sky, whose electromagnetic field generates a perpetual musical tone akin to the voice of God.

When Schumann first made his discovery of the resonant field, it fell into the lap of a physician, Dr. Ankermueller, who suggested the possible relationship between the frequency band of Earth's resonance with the alpha wave patterns of human and mammalian brains. A third scientist, Dr. Herbert Konig, demonstrated in subsequent experiments that the mean average frequency of Schumann resonance was 7.83 Hz, representing a high-end theta and low-end alpha state. In terms of its impact on consciousness, brainwave entrainment with the resonant field of the earth would translate as a light meditative state of wakefulness and relaxation. The resonant cavity of our skull is activated by our voice in a way that can alter and sustain sympathetic brainwave patterns. Singing with devotion, we can imagine our breath as the winds of Earth, our saliva as the oceans and rivers, our tongue the fiery element, collaborating in a reenactment of the supreme and original activity of creation. The relationship between earth's resonant field and the human voice is self-evident. Our bodies are microcosmic reflections of the planetary macrocosm. Like the humming of Earth's resonant field, our voice can generate a frequency that entrains and stabilizes brainwave states, while at the same time massaging our organs, and at the cellular level introducing cymatic order to biological processes.

Sacred songs are a universal component of the world's many spiritual traditions, presumably because of the physical and spiritual benefits just described. Visionary artwork closely resembling the geometric forms of cymatics has emerged from the Shipibo-Conibo tribe of the Amazon. They describe their art as *visual music*, inspired primarily by work with a psychoactive brew of plant medicine called *ayahuasca*. These impressive patterns of shape and color are said to represent direct transmissions from the spirit of the Peruvian rainforest. Accompanying the visual forms are sacred songs called *icaros*, and according to the Shipibo, luminous patterns of geometric energy, which they call *mareacion*, travel through the sonic carrier wave of the *icaro*, generating a resonant field of healing energy in the body that benefits both the shaman who sings it and the community of practitioners that listen. These healing songs and the sacred visual art that accompanies them appear to the shaman simultaneously, as gifts from individual plant spirits. They are believed to impart wisdom, purify dark spirits and dark energies, offer protection, and oversee the outcome of a ceremony. Every living thing is believed to have an *icaro* that can be intuitively channeled with the assistance of ayahuasca.

There appears to be a correlation between the philosophical/theological idea of an original **Word of God** and the emergence of geometric structures on the Earth plane. Visual patterns generated by cymatic technologies illustrate this principle clearly. Furthermore, the sound frequency propagated by our planet's interface with the atmosphere, what scientists call the Schumann resonance, matches the naturally occurring low-alpha brainwave states in human beings, suggesting that our neurology is closely connected to the acoustic aura of Earth.

Through song and prayer, we can vibrate different energy centers of our body, especially the skull and brain, to effectively alter our own brainwave states, which in turn effects how we think and feel, along with the kind of life experiences we attract. The earth-based mystery traditions of indigenous people like the Shipibo-Conibo tribe show how work with plant medicine can assist in the process, bringing "visual music" in through our psychic channels as vibrational medicine with healing applications to ceremonial work. According to the hermetic-alchemical worldview, plants derive their intelligence from subtle astrological influences upon Earth and from the energy of the local ecology, receiving and transmit the "Harmony of the Spheres" by way of their genetic code, aiding us in the gradual discovery of our True Nature.

Reversing Cause and Effect: The Pre-Physical Sound Worlds

Speculative musicologist Marius Schneider proposed a number of stages in the creation process of our material universe. The stage immediately preceding the physical domain was portrayed as a vital world of *pure sound*, a space filled with sound forms that resemble the movements of water, the voice of animals, the rustling of leaves, and so forth. Schneider suggests that the airborne pressure waves we call "sound" are simply an embodied reflection of some higher dimensional reality, and that the material reality we regard as a causal source of nature's sound-effects is, in fact, the *consequence* (i.e. lower-dimensional image and cross-section) of activities taking place within that higher, etheric soundscape. As precursors to the material world, these sound forms are literally out-of-the-ordinary, in that they are non-identical with what we typically think of as ordinary, audible noise.

By this revelatory and theophanic logic, our perception of any physical sound, which by conventional standards would appeared to be "caused" by the interaction between physical "objects", should actually be understood in reverse order. Schneider offers the example of clapping hands. According to his model of the sound world, an upper-dimensional sound *resembling* a handclap brings our hands together in unison as a way of expressing itself. The standing wave patterns of physical form as we know it exist only as a cymatically orchestrated, unfolding energy pattern shaped by a wave-guide of primordial sound, causing these sonically sculpted *clapping hands* to manifest in their lower-dimensional physical analog. All the world's song and sound can be understood as the cooperation of etheric sound-forms and their desire for expression in material form. Not only that, but it would appear that the universe wishes to experience its own sound gestures through the perceptions of sentient nervous systems, as they are designed precisely and ingeniously to enable these very perceptions to occur.

Music informs biological life not only at the level of individual bodies, but also in the harmonized, synchronistic, and morphogenetic field of collaborative species dynamics. One way of grasping this idea is through a study of human language and speech. Thoughts are formulated in our mind prior to their expression as sound. We speak in our mind before we speak with our voice. Words do not begin in the brain but rather in a nonlocal field of collective intelligence, as creative impulses and thought forms waiting to find expression through the physical medium. Ultimately, nothing originates in the brain, whose role is as a local transceiver linked up to the nonlocal field, orchestrating everything from behind the veil of our experiential hologram.

According to Schneider's theory of a formative sound plane, the mammalian ear would have emerged from our planetary evolutionary matrix in service to the ontologically primary world of tone and rhythmic vibrations. Our organs of perception, of which the ear is included, would be cymatically shaped by the same higher-dimensional primordial sounds that orchestrate the handclap. They give shape to our body so as to gather, focus and funnel physical sounds into the human microcosm, invoking an inner-subjective experience of sonic sensuality. How exactly this happens is one of the central mysteries of existence and is presently beyond science's capacity to answer. Cognitive scientists David Chalmers coined an expression, the *hard problem of consciousness*, to describe the mystery of how sensations acquire qualitative characteristics. In contrast to the easy questions (mechanistic models of cognitive functions), answers to the hard problem of consciousness have not been found in our observing physical events in the brain. Consciousness, which is both the source and recipient of these sounds, would have created the mammalian body as a way of temporarily hiding from itself in the guise of an organic life form, so as to self-reflect through the medium of its own creative product.

Few of us, when questioned about the methods of creating and experiencing musical meaning, are able to say anything definitive about it. We only know that music moves us in deep ways. We don't necessarily know *why* it works, nor do we need to know why in order to receive its benefits and blessings. There is a bounty of interesting questions to ask about the mystery of music. Clearly, the way we phrase our inquiry will determine the kind of answers we get. This book aims to articulate some of the ways in which music and cosmos intersect symbolically to produce such spectacular effects upon human consciousness. We will continue to explore music as a harmonizing principle in the human psyche and philosophical current in the lineage of alchemical art. An application of the alchemical worldview to music can unlock *new ways of listening* that acknowledge and shed light upon the deepest and darkest areas of our being.

Our ancestors conceived of music as a profound, auditory gateway into principles of consonance, harmony, balance and proportion. This notion has been challenged over the past century by a heightened presence of dissonance and noise in every area of music composition. Yet if we understand that these post-modern forms of artistic expression represent a creative response to classical notions of harmony, we may come to appreciate discord's place in the musical plenum, as if the evolution of Western music has demanded from its composers an integration of ever-greater orders of harmonic complexity and dissonance over time, pushing the edges of the allowable ever further into the unknown.

TONE COLOR ALCHEMY

ASTROMUSIK represents an effort to describe the basic philosophical premise of the Tone Color Alchemy method. One could compare the musical notes of this system to the buttons on a video game controller – pressing the "X" button may cause your character to jump in one game and punch or kick in another. The same game-controller and game-console can be utilized to elicit completely different activities on the screen. It just depends on which game you are playing. Tone Color Alchemy uses musical notes like controller-buttons, triggering and evoking a chain of magical correspondences each time a note is intoned. Different magical systems may attribute different elements to these same musical notes. Not a problem. We recognize the *relativity* of all magical models and believe that magical practice derives its true power from the internal energy sources of the magician. The mentally constructed systems are just there to help organize certain elements that already exist within one's psyche. They help the individual to focus and bring about significant changes in their life in accordance with their true will.

Of course, magic can be fun, but to dismiss it as *merely a game* would be dangerous and misleading. When working with ritual magic one ought to be cautious, as the effects of this practice are potentially life changing. What makes the Golden Dawn, B.O.T.A., and Tone Color Alchemy correspondences so effective, in my opinion, is their internal and self-referential cohesion. Despite the disagreements that may occur between different magical systems, these tone color attributions were designed with a high degree of *intratextual congruency* that most other "new age" magical systems tend to be seriously lacking.

The original Greek myth of the Harmony of the Spheres correlated musical tones to planets, much like the Tone Color Alchemy system does. However, within their lineage there were several different planetary-note attributions, so that in one system a whole musical scale would correspond to only one planet, whereas in another system each note corresponded to its own planet. Even those systems that attributed planets to individual notes would tend to differ from one theorist to the next, so that the same note could imply Saturn or the Moon depending on whom you took to be the authority. Over the centuries, magicians continued to create magical systems that connected music to the heavens, but never with any kind of consensus. This is precisely why the Tone Color Alchemy correspondences are presented modestly and without any claims to Absolute Truth. New Age literature is saturated with snake oil belief-systems, qualifying the absolute truth of their signal with appeals to the authority of channeled entities and angels. Let's not fall into that trap, shall we?

Musical Cryptography and Magick

Manly P. Hall, in his landmark book *The Secret Teachings of All Ages*, references an essay published anonymously in 1641 called "The Secret and Swift Messenger". The document describes a method of musical cryptography where alphabet letters are translated into musical notes, so that one could conceivably compose a secret message disguised as sheet music. Only the intended recipient would have the translational key to decipher the song and read the intended words. While the Tone Color Alchemy attributions are not intended for cryptographic communication between human agents, they certainly *could* be used that way. Each musical note corresponds to a number of other languages, including the Hebrew alphabet, so that one could conceivably write a message in their native tongue and translate it phonetically into Hebrew, which could in turn be translated into musical notes.

The true purpose of this correspondence system is a subtler form of musical cryptography, where the operator plays the role of both transmitter and receiver of these "secret messages". Communication takes place between the Ego and Higher Self, the symbolic network providing a multi-channeled vocabulary for articulating one's self-transformative intentions to the subconscious mind.

Tone Color Alchemy differs from the Golden Dawn and B.O.T.A. in the way that it caters to musicians and composers specifically. Rather than merely promoting a pre-existing system of ritual praxis, my vision for this project has always been to derive, through speculative musical philosophy and practical magic, an effective method of songwriting that honors the spiritual and psychological processes of the songwriter. Academic approaches to music theory tend to be anatomical and grammatical but not very creative, as I learned during my brief foray through university education and music fundamentals. I wanted to develop a system of magic that was inspirational and applicable to the common instruments of the West – one that would gently guide the musician's creative process without dictating laws of voice-leading or any particular kind of music genre aesthetic.

The twelve-tone system, artificial and harmonically imperfect as it may be, has become an almost universal tuning method due to the popularity of piano, guitar, and symphonic instruments in general. Similarly, the Western astrological-zodiacal wheel's semi-arbitrary subdivision of the sky into twelve equal parts has become a world famous method of analyzing a person's character and destiny.

Tone Color Alchemy Correspondence Table

TONE COLOR	MAJOR ARCANA	ASTROLOGICAL	HEBREW
E Yellow	FOOL	Uranus	Aleph
E Yellow	MAGICIAN	Mercury	Beth
G# Blue	HIGH PRIESTESS	Moon	Gimel
F# Green	EMPRESS	Venus	Daleth
C Red	EMPEROR	Aries	Heh
C# Red-Orange	HIEROPHANT	Taurus	Vav
D Orange	LOVERS	Gemini	Zayin
D# Orange-Yellow	CHARIOT	Cancer	Cheth
E Yellow	STRENGTH	Leo	Teth
F Yellow-Green	HERMIT	Virgo	Yod
A# Violet	THE WHEEL	Jupiter	Kaph
F# Green	JUSTICE	Libra	Lamed
G# Blue	HANGED MAN	Neptune	Mem
G Blue-Green	DEATH	Scorpio	Nun
G# Blue	TEMPERANCE	Sagittarius	Samekh
A Blue-Violet	DEVIL	Capricorn	Ayin
C Red	TOWER	Mars	Peh
A# Violet	STAR	Aquarius	Tzaddik
B Violet-Red	MOON	Pisces	Qoph
D Orange	SUN	Sun	Resh
C Red	JUDGMENT	Pluto	Shin
A Blue-Violet	WORLD	Saturn	Tav

These correspondences make up the core matrix of the Tone Color Alchemy system. The linearity of the sequence shown in the table above is arranged top-down from the first to last tarot cards of the major arcana. The Hebrew letters on the right-hand column are also in a linear sequence from first to last letter, because this is how the attributions of Hebrew to Tarot are organized. However, the tone colors are non-linear, which is to say they are not arranged chromatically from C to C# to D, etc. They follow their own peculiar logic, based on subtler codes that reveal themselves over time through contemplation and study. The origin of this system, as stated before, was the Hermetic Order of the Golden Dawn during the late 19th and early 20th century. The tone color alchemy wheel on the following page represents this correspondence table as a circular mandala.

Tone Color Alchemy Correspondence Wheel

The attributions featured in this Tone Color Alchemy wheel are identical to those featured in the table on the previous page. The outermost circle features the twelve signs of the zodiac arranged in a counterclockwise progression. One layer in you can see the twelve musical notes of the chromatic circle. The next layer features the three outermost planets of our solar system, Uranus Neptune and Pluto, which correspond to Air Water and Fire. One layer deeper is the set of seven planets, including the Sun and Moon, completing the set of 12 signs and 10 planets. At the center of the mandala is the Kabbalistic rose as described by the Sepher Yetzirah, featuring the 22 Hebrew letters in the 12/7/3 arrangement with a rose cross at its center.

Implications of the Tone Color Alchemy System

The model for cosmogenesis described during the first part of this book synthesizes the Greek notion of a *Harmony of the Spheres* with the Jewish Kabbalistic *Tree of Life*. As a poetic and symbolic representation of Creation, rather than a dogmatic religious icon to be worshipped and defended, I have attempted to show how the Tone Color Alchemy wheel relates to physical and metaphysical spaces. Beginning with the familiar Euclidian space-cube as a model of 3-Dimensional physical reality moving through the 1-dimensional chronological timeline of past, present, and future, all perceptions of the 4-Dimensional space-time matrix filter through the zero point of the cube's center, representing consciousness and awareness. Passing through this monad of perception, we arrive in the 4+Dimensional space of the Tree of Life, whose 22 paths mirror the 22 elements of the Cube. The Tree itself is nested in and derived from the geometry of the Flower of Life and Seed of Life, whose origin is the Circle, and ultimately, the empty-fullness of the Formless Eternal (God).

Moving forward from Eternity to Circle to Seed to Flower to Tree to Cube, we pop back out through the Zero Point and into the familiar 4-D space-time domain. In this way we complete the symbolic loop between receptive and projective Awareness. In daily life, our perception of worldly phenomena appears to come from the six faces of the cube, as if there were some externally existing reality that we were observing objectively. Yet what we perceive happening outside of us is actually happening within us, in the sense that we can only know the world around us through our perception of it, and perception is a wholly inward process.

The Tone Color Alchemy wheel is composed of *qualities* attributed to each of the paths along the upper-dimensional Tree of Life. In contrast to the quantitative physics of the 4-D time-space cube, the Tree represents the core archetypes existing on the Inner Planes. Central to these archetypal attributions are the planets and zodiac signs, representing not only the physical planets of our solar system and galactic disk, but also the deeper formative spiritual influences that caused those astral bodies to take form in the way that they have. The tone colors attributed to the astrological symbols represent an effort to ground the philosophy of the Harmony of the Spheres in an actual musical system of correspondence. The TCA system manages to bridge the gap between Greek and Jewish mysticism, so that the "original word of God" described in genesis takes on deeper musical implications as well. The whole Torah could theoretically be translated into musical notes in this way. In summation, the Tone Color Alchemy project is a tool for meditation and ritual invocation of the archetypal energies already existing in our hearts and minds.

The Musical Mind of Kabbalah

The core premise of 19th century Romanticism was that music was absolutely complete unto itself and required no symbolic interpretation. Ideas or concepts used to describe music were seen as projective overlays that detracted from the primary experience of composing, performing and listening. Yet many of the Romantic composers drew their inspiration from mystical states of consciousness and the deep feelings that accompany them. Therefore, while their attitudes bordered on nihilism, they also smacked of a kind of closet mysticism, as if the dominant scientific-materialist paradigm had driven Spirit deep into hiding. Their opposition to representational descriptions of the music served as a defense against the intellectual tendency to reduce gnosis to the printed word.

If music derived its power from anything, according to Absolute Music, it was the temporal and geometric relationships between the notes, which could be described accurately without detracting from the music. Like the fluid and ephemeral play of sunlight upon a body of water, the relationship between spiritual light and the flow of sonic waveforms evoked emotions and visionary states in the listener that were non-prescriptive but nevertheless real. The harmonic and melodic progressions found in music have always been and will always be the result of experimentation with the evocation and juxtaposition of individual notes.

Jewish mysticism, as expressed through the methods of Kabbalah, shares a remarkably similar sentiment to the Absolutists. Despite their deep conviction that the Hebrew alphabet is the most sacred language in existence and that the letters constitute the basic building blocks of Creation, the final purpose of Kabbalistic meditation upon the letters is to arrive at emptiness and consciousness of Nothing. Through endless contemplation upon the letters, the alphanumeric codes of the Torah are a means to an end, a method of purifying one's perceptions so as to achieve union with God, and more generally, to embody wholeness and goodness in everyday life.

There is a critical difference between Kabbalah and Absolute music, however. The latter seeks to express an evocative but intellectually meaningless musical text, whereas **Kabbalah seeks to fill itself so completely with intellectual interpretations of a sacred text that it exhausts itself in the process, satiating the mental desire for meaning and arriving at Emptiness**. These mystical meditations upon the Torah offer an excellent metaphor for the intersection between music composition and Kabbalah via the Tone Color Alchemy method. Through the techniques of *gematria, notariqon,* and *temura,* one derives meanings from music that would otherwise never have occurred to the listener (or composer!)

Gematria: Kabbalah's Alphanumeric Codes

The first Kabbalistic technique that bears mentioning is called **Gematria**. One may use gematria to convert Hebrew letters into numbers by way of alphanumeric correspondences. In ancient times, prior to the integration of the Arabic numerals zero through nine, the Jews and Greeks both did arithmetic with their alphabet letters. Thus each letter had its own numerical value, and when these letters were combined to spell a word, their individual numerical values combined to create a sum total number for that word. A simple example would be the two-lettered Hebrew word for heart (LV = לו = 30 + 6 = 36), which has a value of 36. This may be the earliest known example of linking a single symbolic language (Hebrew) to multiple simultaneous meaning-matrices (letters and numbers). The Tone Color Alchemy correspondence table represents a far more elaborate variation on this original alphanumeric technique.

When Jewish mystics contemplate the Torah, they go far beyond the surface level of the text. They do not merely regard the stories told in the Torah as symbolic and allegorical. The numerical value of words are calculated and cross-referenced. Words with the same value are considered resonant with one another. In an earlier segment of this book I pointed out how the Hebrew letter *Gimel* (גמל) adds up to 73, the same alphanumeric value attributed to the second sphere on the Tree of Life, *Chokmah* (חכמה). Therefore, the number 73 becomes a reference-point of significance. The word *boa* (בעא) means "to pray" and *azn'yah* (אזניה) means "Yah's ear". These two words each add up to 73 as well, and from this chain of associations with the number 73 we derive a Kabbalistic thought-poem - something like a melody. **When we pray, God listens**. This is symbolized both by *gimel* and *Chokmah* in different ways; Chokmah is the second sphere on the Tree of Life, representing **Wisdom** derived from Kether, while gimel is the path connecting Kether to Tiphareth, symbolizing the psycho-spiritual link between **Mind and Heart**.

One of the laws of Gematria is the principle of reduction. Any number containing more than one digit can be **reduced to a single digit** by adding up all the numbers that compose it. For example, 73 = 7+3 = 10 = 1+0 = 1. A Kabbalist might interpret this to represent the original state of Kether, the first sphere. The one who prays to God becomes one with God. The numbers 7 and 3 also represent the first two layers of the Kabbalistic Rose (mother letters and double letters), suggesting the first and second emanations of the Hebrew alphabet. This *twofold value* links in with Chokmah (*second sphere* of the tree) and Gimel (*Key 2* in the major arcana). The Kabbalistic rose is a threefold design, not two-fold, and thus 73 also connects to a sense of incompleteness. The Hebrew word *golem* (גלם=73) appears in Psalms 139:16 and means "my unshaped form", implying a human being who is unfinished in the eyes of God. According to legend, only when one of the Names of God, the *shem*, was *written on a piece and inserted into the golem's head* would it gain life and become active. In a similar way, Gimel and Chokmah would be nothing without Kether, the crown of the Tree of Life from which they both derive their power.

Kabbalistic word play can give rise to a wealth of semantic cross-pollination. It has been said that these activities increase intelligence and purify obscurations in our stream of consciousness. The central tenet of gematria is that something evil can be transmuted into something good by way of naming it and contextualizing it through the spiritual technology of Kabbalah and the Tree of Life. In Kabbalah, there are three basic rules:

Rule 1: Everything connects to everything else.

Rule 2: Everything mirrors everything else.

Rule 3: Encoded in everything is the pattern of everything else.

When we think about something long enough we can eventually see everything else within it. Like the Buddhist idea of **Indra's Net,** symbolized by a spider web that collects moisture from the early morning air, each dewdrop of information contains the reflection of all the others, which in turn contains the reflection of all the others, ad infinitum. This is the nature of gematria. Every word connects to every other one by way of reflective interconnectivity and the Holographic Grid. Paul Foster Case taught that "All the energy that ever was and ever will be is here now" and Einstein's law of the conservation of energy states that energy is neither created nor destroyed.

Gematria is the ultimate solvent of categorical thought and the rational mind, **using the intellect to dissolve the intellect** and bring energy down from the head to the heart through prayer and meditation.

In the Tone Color Alchemy system, each musical tone corresponds to a Hebrew letter and a gematria value. The art of gematria is therefore directly applicable to the current study. Yet its techniques extend beyond the alphanumeric limits of Hebrew to include affiliations with tarot, astrology, color, and music notes. Because our focus is upon music rather than kabbalah, we can re-appropriate our attention to the harmony of the spheres and devise a **gematria of song,**

Alphanumeric Translation Index
ENGLISH and HEBREW

English	Hebrew	Number	English	Hebrew	Number
A	א	1	O	ו/ע	70
B	ב	2	P	פ	80
C	כ/ק	20/100	Q	ק	100
CH	ח	8	R	ר	200
D	ד	4	S	ס	60
E	ה	5	Sh	ש	300
F	פ/ו	6/80	T	ט	9
G	ג	3	Th	ת	400
H	ה	5	Tz	צ	90
I	י	10	U	ו	6
J	י	10	V	ו	6
K	כ	20	W	ו	6
L	ל	30	X	ח/צ	90/8
M	מ	40	Y	י	10
N	נ	50	Z	ז	8

A table similar to this one, featuring all the same correspondences, was laid out in Lon Milo Duquette's book "*The Chicken Qabalah of Rabbi Lamed Ben Clifford*". The table is relatively simple to understand. There are twenty-six English letters and twenty-two Hebrew letters, so that some English letters share the same Hebrew letter. Also, some Hebrew letters represent sounds that don't exist in English and have therefore been added to the list for the sake of accuracy. You can use this table as a reference point if you wish to convert English words into Hebrew. Once these letters have been translated, you can map them onto the tree of life and invoke all of the Tone Color Alchemy attributions, effectively turning words into music notes.

Notariqon & Temurah: Acronyms, Anagrams & Substitutions

The alphanumeric codes of **gematria** create a baseline for further exploration of Kabbalah. Its twin siblings, the techniques of **notariqon** and **temurah**, apply what in English would commonly be called *acronyms*, *anagrams* and *substitutions*, modifying the words and phrases of holy texts to arrive at a revelatory, occult subtext whose deepest meaning is non-dual, non-conceptual, and based on the simple recognition that, as Consciousness, we are intimately connected to everything in the known and unknown universe.

Notariqon works like a verbal accordion. With this technique, the Kabbalist compresses a phrase into a single word or expands a word into a whole phrase. One famous example of Notariqon is found in the word **vitriol**, a sulfuric acid used as a corrosive agent in ancient alchemical work as well as modern chemistry. Magicians attributed the phrase "Visita Interiora Terrae Rectificando Invenies Occultum Lapidem" to its abbreviated form as the acronym V.I.T.R.I.O.L., translating as "Visit the interior of the Earth, by rectification you shall find the hidden stone." Vice versa, individual words can be unfolded into a string of words. The first word of Genesis, Beresheit (בראשית), for example, expands into the phrase *"Beresheit Rah Elohim Shiqblv Israel Torah"* which translates as "In the beginning Elohim saw that Israel would accept the law".

These two modes of Notariqon, compression and expansion, can be applied to musical notes as well, where a horizontal, melodic series could be expanded vertically so that each musical note becomes the root or base note of a chord harmony. This is an especially valuable tool in the Tone Color Alchemy method because it allows the individual greater creative freedom. In the image below you can see how a simple melody, the C Major Scale, can be converted by way of Notariqon into a series of harmonic chord forms. Each note of the melody becomes the root of a chord triad, depending on its position in the scale and the intervals formed through stacking thirds diatonically. However, the same melody could be harmonized any number of ways. It's up to you!

Musical Notariqon

Temurah is the third and final technique of Kabbalistic word play, accomplished through the shuffling and/or substitution of letters in a word to arrive at new words. The anagram method of temurah is supported by the logic of gematria, in the sense that a word's letters will add up to the same value no matter what order they are arranged in. Earlier in this book I showed how the anagrams "Notes, Tones, and Stone" reveal different facets of the same phenomenon, tones representing physical vibrations and notes representing our own mentally formulated symbols of the tones. This same kind of thought process was applied to Hebrew words in the Old Testament as a way of enriching one's relationship to a word, phrase, or concept.

א:1 , י:10 , ק:100	ב:2, כ:20, ר: 200	ג:3, ל:30, ש:300
ד:4, מ:40 ת:400	ה:5, נ:50	ו:6, ס:60
ז: 7, ע: 70	ח: 8, פ: 80	ט: 9, צ: 90

THE NINE CHAMBERS (AIQ BKR)

In addition to the anagram method, Temurah can signify a substitution of letters with other letters, the logic of these substitutions varying depending on the method employed. One common technique of Temurah is called the Nine Chambers, or in Hebrew, AIQ BKR[15]. The nine chambers refer to the numerals one through nine and their corresponding alphabet letters. For example, the letters Aleph, Yod, and Qoph have gematria values of 1, 10, and 100, so they belong to the first chamber. The letters Beth, Kaph, and Resh represent 2, 20, and 200 in the second chamber. This same pattern continues through all nine chambers and includes all 22 letters.

The application of Temurah to tonal music is twofold; **anagrams** correspond to *melodic variation*, where the same notes of a melody can be reorganized at the whim of the composer to produce new melodic sequences. Anagrams also apply to *chord voicings and inversions*, where the vertical order of pitches in a chord may be rearranged to describe the same basic chord, only in different interval positions. **Substitution** corresponds to *modulation*, whereby a melody or harmonic progression may be transposed into other keys, maintaining their intervallic structure but moving into lower or higher pitch registers. A song written in the Key of C, for example, could be transposed into the Key of C# by shifting all of the harmonic and melodic intervals simultaneously up one half step.

---

[15] For a description of how the nine chambers correspond to the nine planetary magic squares, see Lon Milo Duquette's book "*Chicken Qabalah*".

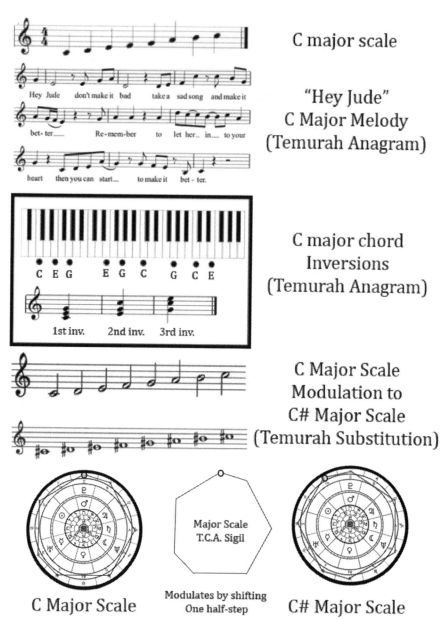

C major scale

"Hey Jude"
C Major Melody
(Temurah Anagram)

C major chord
Inversions
(Temurah Anagram)

C Major Scale
Modulation to
C# Major Scale
(Temurah Substitution)

C Major Scale

Major Scale
T.C.A. Sigil

Modulates by shifting
One half-step

C# Major Scale

At the top is a simple C major scale, followed by an example of how the notes of a scale, or of any melodic phrase for that matter, can be shuffled to create new melodies, just like the letters of a word can be shuffled around to create new words. The same applies vertically with regards to the order of notes in a chord harmony.

The Lesser Banishing Ritual of the Pentagram

Hermetic Order of the Golden Dawn

The Kabbalistic techniques of meditation just described are primarily introspective and contemplative, representing only one half of practice in the Western hermetic tradition. Through *gematria, notariqon, and temurah*, the practitioner discovers words of power that can be incorporated into ritual magic. Ceremonial embodiment of magical thought represents the other half of the practice, bringing the personal will into alignment with one's Holy Guardian Angel. In Golden Dawn ceremonial magic, some preliminary steps must be taken before attempting the more advanced works of invocation and conversation with the HGA. Central to this preparation is the Lesser Banishing Ritual of the Pentagram, or LBRP, a ritual designed to energetically clear a space and ensure that one is safe to proceed with further work.

Paul Foster Case, the first person to publicly disclose what I have termed "tone color alchemy" correspondences, was a high-ranking initiate of the Thoth-Hermes lodge of Alpha et Omega, which was itself a branch of the Golden Dawn founded in 1906. His background as a musician and composer, along with his advanced understanding of western hermetic philosophy and ritual practice, granted him a special appreciation for the musical elements of rituals taught to him through the Thoth-Hermes lodge. The performance of LBRP could be fine-tuned through the application of musical notes to individual Hebrew letters. Holy names invoked during the banishing ritual were sung according to these correspondences.

Israel Regardie, serving as a source of accurate information regarding the Golden Dawn's inner teachings, wrote one of the most influential magical texts of this lineage during the 20th century, called "*The Middle Pillar*". In this book, Regardie describes the Lesser Banishing Ritual of the Pentagram in detail, along with a number of other critical visualizations for novice magicians first discovering the Golden Dawn. Originally published in 1938, the text was edited and updated a number of times, the third edition being published in 1995 and featuring an afterword by Thom Parrott entitled "*The Musical Qabalah*". In this short chapter, Parrott claims that the origin of the tone color attributions taught by Paul Case were actually sourced in another member of the Golden Dawn, Allan Bennett, who had served as a teacher for famous occultists Aleister Crowley and Dion Fortune. This claim seems to be corroborated by Case in his book "*Correlation of Sound and Color*", page 4, where he alludes to the previous secrecy of these teachings and their safekeeping in the esoteric orders from which he sourced them. The true origins of these tone-color relationships in the Golden Dawn remains a mystery, as is the case with much content in these fraternal secret societies. Nevertheless, we can make practical use of the tone-colors thanks to the work of people like Case and Parrott, who offered diagrams in their books similar to what I have illustrated on the following page.

Ah - Tah - Ah   Mm   Al   Ku   Oo   Th   Ve   Ge   Bu   Oo   Ra   Ah

א   ת   ה   מ   ל   כ   ו   ת   ו   ג   כ   ו   ר   ה

ATAH   MALKUTH   VE GEBURAH

Ve   Ge   Du   Oo   La   Ah   Le   Aa   Oh   La   Am   Ah   Mm   En

ו   ג   ד   ו   ל   ה   ל   ע   ו   ל   ם   א   מ   נ

VE GEDULAH   LE OLAHM   AMEN

Details regarding the full method and purpose of the LBRP can be found in numerous books on Western ceremonial magick. Pitch register is not prescribed by the attributions, and so these names could be sounded in any octave. I have chosen to omit specifics of the LBRP from this text, only touching on the musical aspect of the ceremony, and even then, I have only shown here what previous teachers have already made publically available. In this way I hope to honor the Golden Dawn lineage and create a safeguard against premature exposure to the Work. The holy names shown above are intoned during the **Qabalistic Cross**, the first segment of the ritual.

As you can see, the names were originally given through the Hebrew language, each letter converted by way of the Tone-Color attributions into musical notes, so that the magician could chant the names with musical precision. Musicians who scrutinize the melodies will notice that they are atonal and disjunctive in their contour. This is a common quality among most of the melodies and harmonic forms generated with the Tone Color Alchemy Method. Over the years, I have developed a greater appreciation for the harmonic beauty of the major and minor scales, which rarely emerge through the chance operations of alpha-tonal conversions such as the ones above.

Composing Music from Seed Melodies

What really differentiates the Tone Color Alchemy method from Paul Foster Case and the Golden Dawn's system of magic is its application to music composition and songwriting. Drawing upon these archetypal attributions as inspiration for sculpting sound, we can consciously project and connect our psychic energy to melodic and harmonic forms in a methodical way. Most musicians do this naturally, getting in touch with their feelings and experimenting with ways of programming these feels into sound frequencies. Unlike other methods of music theory, which attempt to define laws of voice leading and chord phrasing for the musician, sculpting styles of composition according to their own aesthetic and harmonic biases, the Tone Color method opens up a multidimensional playing field and enriches the associative meanings of music without telling the composer what kind of chord, progressions and melodies to can work with. Tonality and atonality are equally permissible.

Despite the open-ended harmonic parameters of this practice, there are some basic guidelines of songwriting that apply and may be useful to mention here. When the letters of a word are translated into a string of musical notes, any number of techniques could be applied to develop it into a full song. I like to think of these notes as a **Seed Melody**, as if the notes make up a kind of genetic code that shape the growth of the song. Depending on the nutrient density of the soil, light and water exposure, and other plants hanging out in the local ecology, a seed will express its potential to varying degrees. In a similar way, the development of a seed melody is a function of the songwriter who works with it.

A sacred name can be translated into musical notes to form a seed melody. This first phase is purely translational and requires no creative intuition, in the sense that one only has to refer to a conversion table to complete the task. Once we have a seed melody to work with, the next phase in the process is to go to a musical instrument, usually a keyboard or guitar, to play the notes and see how they naturally evolve. The songwriter may hear certain chords under the notes before a rhythm becomes apparent, or the reverse, a rhythm may appear that can then be harmonized and elaborated upon. Therefore, the creative process is not necessarily a linear and formulaic one, however it does tend to sprout from the seed melody to a rhythmic and harmonically endowed musical motif.

Over time, through contemplation of the seed notes and sprouting motif, one will eventually realize a number of available options and directions in which the piece could grow to arrive at its fully realized potential.

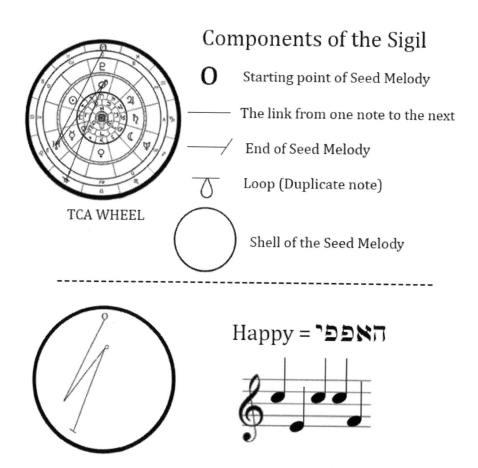

Components of the Sigil

O   Starting point of Seed Melody

———   The link from one note to the next

——⁄   End of Seed Melody

     Loop (Duplicate note)

     Shell of the Seed Melody

TCA WHEEL

Happy = הַאפפי

Any word can be shaped into a seed melody and sigil. The basic components of musical sigils are presented in the image above. The starting point of the melody, corresponding to the first letter of the word, is marked by the presence of a circle. The letters that come after it are identified by a linear progression from point to point along the nodes of the TCA wheel. For example, the letters H-A-P-P-Y correspond to the Hebrew letters הַאפפי (Aries, Uranus, Mars, Mars, and Virgo), each of which has their own designated position on the wheel. The repeat letter P is indicated by a loop and the final letter Y is marked by a perpendicular line, symbolically cutting off the flow of energy and closing the code-circuit. Once the sigil has been formed, it is stored in a circle, like the husk or shell of a seed serving as a container for its contents. How you plant and nourish the seed's development is up to you, the songwriter-composer.

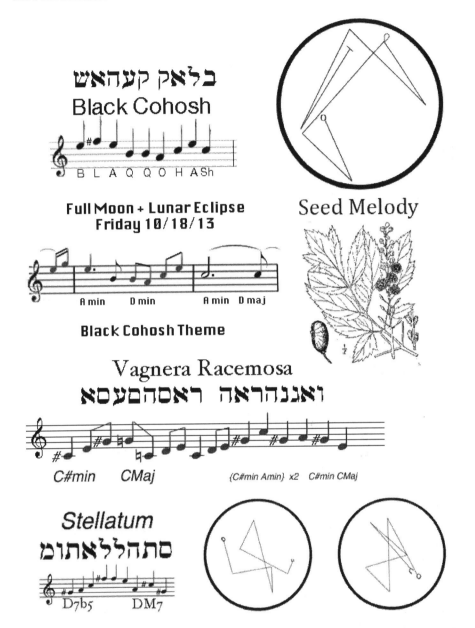

בלאק קעהאש
Black Cohosh

B L A Q Q O H ASh

**Full Moon + Lunar Eclipse
Friday 10/18/13**

A min   D min   A min   D maj

Black Cohosh Theme

Seed Melody

Vagnera Racemosa
ואגנהראה ראסהםעסא

C#min   CMaj   {C#min Amin} x2   C#min CMaj

Stellatum
סתהלללאתום

D7b5   DM7

In this example, the first seed melody was derived from the name of a plant called Black Cohosh and incorporated into a full-moon lunar eclipse ritual from October of 2013. An herbalist friend later gave me two more plants to work with, vagnera racemosa and stellatum, which I converted into notes and integrated into the piece.

Musemes: Geometric Musical Archetypes

When we hear the word "archetype" in a psychological context, we tend to think of psychic energy patterns dressed up in transcultural, mythological themes. The hero archetype, for example, shows up in myths all over the world, although the names, appearance, and adventures of the hero will differ from one story to the next. Likewise, the "evil villain" archetype usually appears in the hero's journey to test their resolve, and in many of the traditional hero myths, the villain presents obstacles toward the attainment of something sacred, such as a knight's search for the Holy Grail or the rescuing of a damsel in distress. Whatever the particular details of the story may be, there are transcultural themes that consistently show up and can easily be identified, not only in fictional tales but also in the events of our every day lives. As we become more aware of life's story-like quality, we can begin to script our own personal story so that it resonates with the fundamental narrative patterns of our collective human mythos.

Working with the definition of archetypes as subtle, psychic energy patterns, we could frame the "magic of music" as a confluence of archetypal energies that find expression in and through the sound domain. **Musical spirits**, if we can speak of such things, would be found in the same world of archetypal elements familiar to the great storytellers and visual artists. This particular kind of musical spirit, or musical archetype, is hinted at in an earlier chapter on Absolute Music where I describe the Romantic belief that music existed totally separate from any of its audible forms.

A second category of musical archetype is one that, rather than being defined by hidden energy patterns in the human psyche, is defined by the geometric structure of a musical sequence, and regarded as independent of any emotional or mythic context. It is not at all uncommon that songwriters use the same melodic device to communicate entirely different feelings. Musicologists have coined a term, the **museme** (musical-theme), to define a minimal unit of musical meaning in terms of linguistics rather than psychology. Much like the string of notes in a seed-sigil, the museme is like a small molecule or biological cell that if broken down any further would cease to express its most basic structural role in the composition.

In the example that follows, I give an example of how one museme could appear in three unrelated songs, even in different keys, while still expressing the same basic geometric form. This particular museme is composed of five notes. Modulation from one key to another is achieved by clockwise or counter-clockwise rotations of the seed-sigil upon the surface of the unmoved Tone color Alchemy wheel.

Recurring Musical Motifs as Spiritual Entities

Museme Sigils and Modulation

EXAMPLE No.1

Motif: First Four ascending notes of Locrian mode
are played in sequence followed by a return to the
first note.

1) PAUL MCCARTNEY, Ram, "Long Haired Lady" 0:36-0:45

D Locrian followed B Locrian

2) CHRONO TRIGGER OST, "End of Time" theme, 0:55-0:59

A Locrian

3) FANTASTIC PLANET (1973) Soundtrack: 29:02-31:08

A Locrian followed by G Locrian

**Locrian Motif
Seed Sigil**

Chord Modulation:

**Whole
Step
60°
Rotation**

Counter-Clockwise

A Locrian Motif

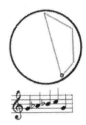

G Locrian Motif

Recurring Museme Melodies in Video Game Music

Warp Whistles and the Ocarina of Time

EXAMPLE No.2

Motif: This melodic sequence was composed by Japanese videogame songwriter, Koji Kondo, and used as a theme for the title track of Zelda: The Ocarina of time as well as the "Warp Whistle" theme of Super Mario Bros. 3. Here we come closer to the ideal "archetypal musical theme" in that both melodies imply a musical instrument used by the main character to time travel and open dimensional portals to other worlds.

The melody is composed of six musical notes played above two Major 7 chords. In relation to both the IV and I chords, the melody touches the major 7th note implied by the chord beneath it. It also features a chromatic descent, deviating from the strict and traditional boundaries of harmony. An identical melody appears during the opening theme to Chrono Trigger, another popular video game from the 90's, though it was composed by another person (Yasunori Mitsuda) and is harmonized with an E minor 7 chord rather than the previous two major 7 chords.

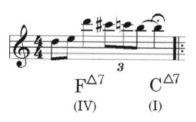

Mario Bros 3 (Warp Whistle Theme)
+
Zelda: Ocarina of Time (Main Theme)

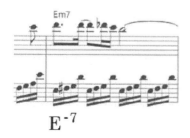

Chrono Trigger (Main Theme)

1:00-1:07

ZEBRAXAS

"I am beginning to see in my mind's eye, Zebra itself, an actual animal, a striped horse. Shy and merry and mischievous, half hiding in the forest at the far edge of the Heide, the sun shining, and Zebra playfully advancing and then just when you think he's going to emerge fully and separate himself from the trees, suddenly and unexpectedly he retreats and absolutely vanishes ... You can't coax him out, or lure him; you can't get your hands on him. His white is the dazzle of the sun; his dark stripe the shadows in the glade and forest, where, amid the shadowy green / the little things of the forest live unseen." –
The Exegesis of Phillip K. Dick

! ABRAHADABRA !

! ABRAXAS !

! ABRA !

! BRA !

! RA !

! A !

Who is this elusive spirit of light and shadow that P.K.D. calls **Zebra**? Encoded in the name may be a clue. The final three letters of Zebra, BRA, are the first three letters of beresheit (בראשית), the very first word of Genesis meaning "in the beginning", closely resembling the ancient Aramaic word Abradacadabra, which means, "I create as I speak". A keyword in the lineage of stage magic, abracadabra was reformulated by Crowley as **Abrahadabra** to signify its place in ritual magick as the **Word of the Aeon** and the **Great Work** accomplished.

Pillip K Dick's **Exegesis,** originally composed of almost 8000 pages, documents his lifelong exploration of religious and visionary states.

Arguably the most influential and cutting edge science fiction writer of the 20th century, Dick authored a number of books that were later turned into popular science fiction movies (Blade Runner, Total Recall, Screamers, Minority Report, A Scanner Darkly, etc.).

His journaling, which eventually became the Exegesis, began with a critical date refered to repeatedly in the book as "2-3-74". According to the story, Dick had his wisdom teeth removed and was visited by a delivery person from the pharmacy in early February 1974. He noticed that she was wearing a fish symbol around her neck and so he asked her what it meant. It turns out the symbol was an **Ichthys fish**, a vesica Pisces symbol used by early mystical Christianity to represent Christ. This interaction triggered a profound moment of awakening for Phillip, what he called *anamnesis*, which is a Greek word meaning "loss of forgetfulness".

In the weeks that followed, Dick experienced a number of hallucinations that he contemplated and wrote about in his Exegesis. Described as a slideshow of abstract kaleidoscopic patterns that came from an information-rich **laser beam of pink light**, he named the source of these anamnestic lucidity stimulators **Zebra**, while at other times calling it God and eventually VALIS, an acronym for the phrase "Vast Active Living Intelligence System". The word VALIS later became the title of one of his most popular novel trilogies of the same name.

According to his journals, Dick interpreted Valis as the node of an artificial satellite network that originated from Sirius, the Dog Star of the Canis Major constellation. Earth was also portrayed as a satellite that used pink laser beams for information transference between humanity and an extraterrestrial species, whose aim was to dismantle our tendencies for amnesia and trigger the gnostic recollection of intrinsic universal knowledge. The purpose of our DNA was as a transducer of this pink laser light and as memory coils storing information of our collective memory.

Humanity, according to Dick, is participating in a simulated, holographic reality matrix in which we are trapped. In his book Valis, he makes reference to the Black Iron Prison, his name for the tyrannical and omnipresent control system that seems to be emerging on our planet at this time. Referring to it also as the Empire, Dick proposes that we are all trapped in a trans-temporal reiteration of Rome 70 A.D.

The **Zebra Principle** states that a benign, higher order of inorganic mimicry exists in the universe capable of restructuring human memory and laying down false memory templates to keep us from accurately perceiving it. It casts a plasmatic veil upon the earth, so enormous and all pervasive that we cannot detect it with ordinary vision. An extraterrestrial life form, Zebra came to earth to raise humanity from its maligned condition and to reveal to us the cruel, soul-destroying prison of society that we have created for ourselves. In this way, Zebra plays the role of a gnostic deity, not so different from the Christ figure in its multidimensional benevolence. Despite its great power, Dick says that Zebra is vulnerable and mortal, lending to its understanding, empathy, and compassion for humanity.Philip K Dick's encounter with the Ichthys fish necklace triggered a major spiritual awakening within him, leading to his discovery of the **Zebra Principle**.

Note: An ancient tradition of wearing necklace amulets for protection became popular among early members of the Catholic church, usually inscribed with the word **Ichthys** because it contained the Greek initials for **Jesus Christ**. Similarly, the mystical Christian sects wore stones around their neck, inscribed with the word "Abraxas", each of its seven letters representing one of the seven classical planets. As a **Gnostic-Archonic Deity**, Abraxas ruled over the 365 worlds, the last of which represents those angels who are the authors of our physical world. Refer to the book *The Search for Abraxas* by Nevill Drury and Stephen Skinner for further details.

The Greek alphabet had its own gematria values and alphabet, separate from the Tone Color Alchemy correspondence table. Although I have not included a detailed outline of Greek gematria in this book, suffice to say that the alphanumeric conversion process is more or less the same.

GREEK GEMATRIA:

ICHTHYS (ἰχθύς): Gematria value of **77**

ABRAXAS (ΑΒΡΑΣΑΞ): Gematria value of **365**

ENGLISH GEMATRIA:

ZEBRAXA: Gematria value of **77** (26+5+2+18+1+24+1=77)

HEBREW GEMATRIA:

ZBRAXS: Gematria value of 360 (7+2+200+1+90+60=360)

ZEBRAXS: Gematria value of **365** (7+5+2+200+1+90+60=**365**)

ZEBRAXAS: Gematria value of 366 (7+5+2+200+1+90+1+60=**366**)
Zebraxas (זהבראצאס) represents the passage from a perfect circle (360) to 365 Worlds of ABRAXAS to the New Years Day on Earth (**365+1**)

Z.E.B.R.A.X.A.S. (זהבראצאם)

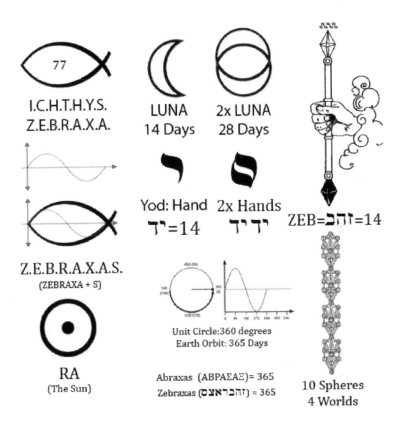

I.C.H.T.H.Y.S.
Z.E.B.R.A.X.A.

LUNA
14 Days

2x LUNA
28 Days

Yod: Hand   2x Hands
י=14   יד יד

ZEB=זהב=14

Z.E.B.R.A.X.A.S.
(ZEBRAXA + S)

RA
(The Sun)

Unit Circle:360 degrees
Earth Orbit: 365 Days

Abraxas (ΑΒΡΑΣΑΞ)= 365
Zebraxas (זהבראצאם) = 365

10 Spheres
4 Worlds

My discovery of the sacred name Zebraxas was intuitive and creative, coming from within rather than without. It is a deeply personal symbol, representing my love for the actual animal as well as Dick's mythological entity. Given that an Ichthys fish necklace triggered discovery of the Zebra Principle, and that my natal sun is in Pisces, it seems inevitable that I would eventually discover the figure of Zebraxas.

In Greek gematria, the value of Abraxas is 365. However, when translated phonetically into Hebrew, Abraxas no longer produces the number 365. Only when we introduce and synthesize the name of the Zebra with Abraxas do we recover the original gematria value of 365. On the following page I will describe the Kabbalistic logic that led me to this particular Hebrew spelling of Zebraxas as זהבראצאם.

A wealth of holographic subtext can be extracted from the divine name of Zebraxas. For example, the Hebrew letters ZEB (זהב) represent the numbers 7+5+2, totaling as the number 14. The tenth letter of the Hebrew alphabet, Yod (י), when spelled out phonetically (יד) equals 10+4=14, putting it in resonance with ZEB. As described in detail earlier in this book, each letter of the Hebrew alphabet becomes a word when it is spelled out, so that Yod י means "hand" and Daleth ד means "door". Thus Yod implies a hand reaching through a door, a familiar symbol in the ace cards of the tarot's minor arcana. The ace of each suit in the deck features a hand reaching through a cloud holding the elemental weapon of that suit. There are four suits in total, composed of ten "pip" cards (ace through ten) and four "royal" cards (page, knight, queen, king), adding to the significance of the number fourteen.

The Greek word Ichthys sums to 77 (7+7=14) and the number 14 has further significance in its connection to the lunar cycles, which are comprised of a 14 day waxing and 14 day waning cycles. The two curves of the vesica are formed by the interior of two lunar crescents in an inverse juxtaposition, representing the twin cycles of increasing and decreasing light during a full lunar month of 28 days. Two Yods can be combined in a similar way to produce a third Yod in the negative space between them, just as the thumb and forefingers of our two human hands form the symbol of Yod when pressed together in the same inverse, reciprocal fashion. Try it!

In English alphanumeric code, "Zebraxa" totals 77, putting it in resonance with the Ichthys symbol, and when we add the final letter S not only to the word Zebraxas but to the fish symbol itself, where S is rotated 90 degrees to represent a Sine Wave, we can see its connection to the previous chapter on sonic cosmogenesis and the unit circle. Composed of 360 degrees, the Unit Circle connects to the Hebrew spelling of Zebraxas when the extraneous vowels are omitted (זברכאצס=360) as is common in the Hebrew language. The Hebrew letter Samekh, which is the letter S in the name Abraxas, is shaped like a unit circle (ס) and in its gematria value of 60, it connects implies one of the six circles encompassed by the seed of life (60x6=360).

The Tree of Life emerges from the Seed of Life, composed of 10 spheres plus 22 paths, for a combined value of 32 Paths. When multiplied by three, signifying the first three Kabbalistic worlds (Atziluth, Briah, and Yetzirah), the number 32 becomes 96, which is the English alphanumeric code for the full name Zebraxas, where **Zebraxa:77 + S:19 = ZEBRAXAS 96,** relating to the aforementioned Gnostic idea of Abraxas as the 365 stages of creation prior to the material world and Zebraxas amounting to the same number.

Adjunct to the lunar attribution of ZEB is the solar attribution of RA, the Egyptian sun deity of Heliopolis. The black and white stripes of the Zebra represent the dark and light phases of the moon, whose light is sourced in the sun. The remaining letters **XAS** are a common acronym in scientific literature for **X-ray absorption Spectrography**, a prevalent technique for identifying the local electro-geometric structure of matter, which is just a fancy way of describing the measurement of X-ray absorption by way of **frequency wavelengths.** Could its name be more perfect?

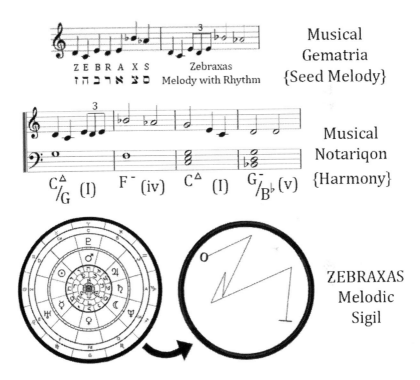

Musical
Gematria
{Seed Melody}

Z E B R A X S   Zebraxas
ז ה ב ר א צ ס   Melody with Rhythm

Musical
Notariqon
{Harmony}

C^{Δ}/G (I) F^{-} (iv) C^{Δ} (I) $G^{-}/B^{\flat}$ (v)

ZEBRAXAS
Melodic
Sigil

Here you can see how the initial conversion process of English letters to Hebrew letters has become a linear series of musical notes. These alphabet-notes, lacking in any rhythmic and harmonic context, function as the **prima materia** of our musical-alchemical experiments. In this particular example I have taken the notes of ZEBRAXAS and with my creative intuition, assigned a rhythm to them to form a **Seed Melody.** From here, I have attributed new base notes to the melody so as to harmonize them, and have intuitively expanded upon the melody with two additional measures so that it comes across as a complete musical theme. The symbols beneath the staff indicate the chord types and their harmonic function.

Who Is the Composer?

If the seed melodies derived through our Tone Color Alchemy conversion table represent a kind of musical genetic code, as pre-determined sequences of notes loosely dictating the harmonic parameters and potentialities of a composition, then the composer represents the environment in which that seed develops from seed to sprout and into maturity. In alchemical language, there are four elements (earth air water fire) that intersect in the material plane to define the seed's environment. A seed needs the soil's darkness and nutrients, water to keep it moist and hydrated, wind to deliver the carbon dioxide that sustains its life, and the light from the fire of the sun for photosynthesis and steady temperature levels. All four of these elements combine to nurture the genetic potential of the seed into fruition.

The human psyche similarly partakes in the four elements during the creative process of songwriting and music composition. In the tarot's minor arcana, the four suits are said to represent these elements in the following way:

PENTACLES	CUPS	SWORDS	WANDS
EARTH	WATER	AIR	FIRE
RHYTHM	HARMONY	MELODY	DYNAMICS

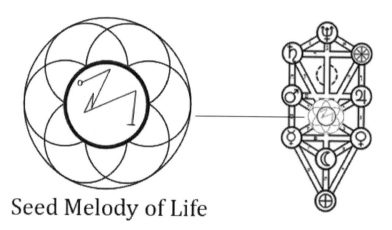

Seed Melody of Life

Musical notes in a seed-melody have not yet been shaped by the elements. They still exist in a state of unexpressed quantum potentiality. A mature human organism embodies these elemental qualities through the autonomic nervous system, which is to say that the health of our physical body has a direct influence on the health of the seed melody that we are working with.

The Human Sensorium and Chakra System

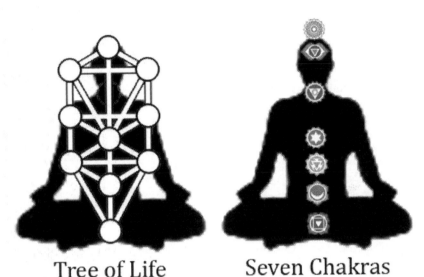

Tree of Life   Seven Chakras

The seed's higher-dimensional code must pass through the filter of our nervous system in order to ground down into physical reality as sonic pressure waves. As this process transpires, the melody is gradually imbued with our soul-energy and develops into a symbolic mirror of our inner condition. The rhythm of our heart, the harmony between our organs, the thought-stream of our mind, and the dynamic passion of our desires all contribute to the quality of the final product.

If a composer constitutes the channel through which a musical seed develops into a fully realized composition, then who or what is the composer? From the elemental perspective, we are composed of archetypal forces whose signature appears in all of the physical and psycho-spiritual layers of our being. The four-element model is one way of tracking this, however it is not the only way. When dealing with the energy systems of the body, one inevitably encounters the Indian notion of a chakra system. Each chakra is like an energetic vortex or spinning wheel, focusing and distributing our life force energy through designated points along the body. Spinning at different frequencies, the root chakra is said to be the slowest and densest, the circulation of each chakra accelerating as one climbs up the spine, so that the crown chakra spins at the highest and fastest frequency.

A Skeptical Look at Musical Notes and the Chakras

The Tree of Life maps onto the energy centers of our physical body, much like the chakra system maps onto the vertical channel of our spine. Malkuth, the lowest sphere on the Tree of Life, relates to the root chakra and the four elements of the physical plane. Climbing up the middle pillar to Yesod, the sphere directly above Malkuth, we find the attribution of the moon, the same "planet" associated with the sacral chakra. The solar plexus of the chakra system falls between Yesod and Tiphareth. The heart chakra relates to the Tiphareth, the center of the three. Da'ath, the hidden sphere between Tiphareth and Kether is attributed to the throat chakra. The mind's eye is positioned at the cross section between Daleth and Gimel. The uppermost point on the skull, the crown chakra, correlates to both Kether and Ain Soph Aur, the egg of limitless light that envelops Kether.

A significant number of New Age authors have, over the past sixty or so years, published their model of the human body and how chakras correspond to musical notes. When I first began exploring metaphysics and its connection to music, I discovered many books that addressed this topic. In my efforts to compare these texts to one another, I hoped to gain some deeper understanding about the relationship between music and the human spirit by way of the physical body. However, this research quickly brought up feelings of frustration and confusion for me, as I realized that each author contradicted the next in their claims about which notes corresponded to which chakras. Not only that, but they often presented the material as if their pet-system were an indisputably true representation of "Reality".

I also noticed that most of the authors writing on this topic didn't know the first thing about music theory; they recognized musical notes as vibrations measured by frequency, and could conceive that each chakra had a periodic frequency, much like the planetary orbital frequencies are attributed to a "harmony of the spheres", but that seemed to be the extent of their musical metaphysics.

It is my personal opinion that the human body *does* have energy centers along the spine and that musical notes *could be* attributed to the chakras of our body. What many authors who write on this topic neglect to mention is the relativity of their own attributions. Everyone's body is different and so it seems as if the speed of their chakras would vary depending on their state of physical health. Would the pitch value of these energetic vortexes not fluxuate from one person to the next? If we wish to say that the root chakra corresponds to "C", the heart chakra to "F#", and so on, then we owe it to ourselves to recognize the artificial nature of these attributions.

Artifice is not necessarily a bad thing. Our clothes and houses are manmade and artificial, yet for most people they are indispensable to daily life. When it comes to inner work, manmade models of Spirit can be just as handy, sheltering us from astral influences and creating a vessel through which we traverse the imaginal realms. However, just as it would be foolish to say that my wardrobe is the *only* clothing that exists, it similarly makes no sense to say that one person's magical attributions are the only ones that exist. That does not mean that my wardrobe doesn't keep me warm and decorated, or that a certain magical system won't strengthen my will and relationship with God. It just seems important to retain a healthy measure of skepticism.

"God is a concept by which we measure our pain." – John Lennon

"God is a concept by which we measure our pleasure" – Anonymous

Claims that certain chakras correspond universally to a certain musical frequency are the symptom of a "one size fits all" mentality, like anatomical illustrations in a book about the human body. The image of the body represents *an example of a body* rather than *the* human body. In reality, if chakras have any existence at all, I imagine that their spin would have a periodic frequency that organically fluxuates within an individual's lifetime, as well as from one person to the next.

I believe that the attribution of certain tones and colors to each chakra could be a truly effective way or working with psychosomatic conditions. Just as hearing the words of our native language induces thoughts and feelings, despite the words themselves amounting to little more than mouth-noises, we can create mental links between sound, color, and physical energies.

Tone Color Alchemy attributions between notes and planets have already been sufficiently established over the course of this book. However, in attempting to solve the riddle of tone color alchemy correspondences to the chakras, I felt compelled to make a clear decision regarding which symbolic language would take priority. Should we go by planets or tone-colors?

On the one hand, planetary attributions represent psychological principles that do seem to constellate with reference to certain areas of the body. However, the idea of a vertical low-to-high frequency gradient in the chakras is also intuitive, where the root is corresponds to the slowest and lowest musical note, while the crown evokes the quickest and highest musical note. Since I didn't come up with the Tone Color Alchemy attributions personally, I feel absolved from the duty of restructuring the system to account for its apparent contradictions. Instead, I will lay out the details of what I am seeing and you can make up your own mind.

Planetary Chakra Attributions

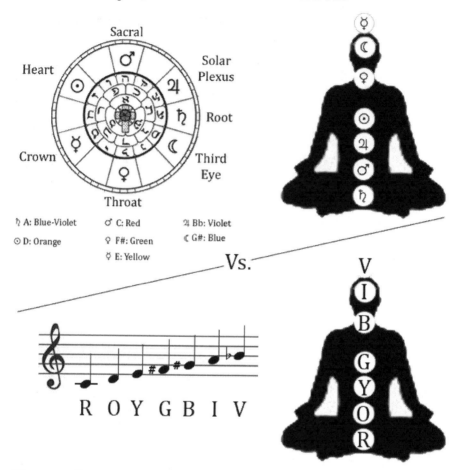

Tone Color Chakra Attributions

The planetary attributions in the upper half of this image represent *one of the many* classical alchemical attributions of planets to the metals, which in turn are said by some researchers to correlate to the Indian chakra system. A stepwise assignment of musical notes to the chakras is more common, arranged as a linear, rainbow gradient of Red, Orange, Yellow, Green, Blue, Indigo, and Violet (ROYGBIV). I suspect that the effectiveness of frequency medicine is essentially a function of belief. In fact, given the numerous contradictory systems that exist and are practiced around the world today, it may be even more accurate to say that the effectiveness of mysticism hinges on the individual's strength in the *suspension of disbelief*.

John Cage - I Ching - Chance Operations

TONE COLOR ALCHEMY DIVINATION

The goal of Tone Color Alchemy is to bring the feeling of **sacred intention** back into the music composition process through methods that offer a high degree of creative and harmonic freedom, integrating the conventional twelve-tone instruments of the West along with their rich astrological history (Harmony of the Spheres). Seed melodies can be derived from sacred names, as demonstrated in previous chapters, however there are still other methods of gathering these seeds without translating names into notes. Many of these methods fall under the umbrella category of divination.

An extension of the root word *"divine"*, divination refers to any spiritual practice where an individual poses a question or contemplates a situation with the intention to gain insight by way of omens and a connection to some divine and supernatural force. In my experience, divination can be effective regardless of whether the individual believes that an actual, separate entity is guiding them, although over time one may begin to suspect that this is in fact the case. The bible forbids all acts of divination by laypersons, but in Exodus makes reference to Urim and Thummim, a form of divination reserved for the priest class, as if to suggesting that divination is dangerous and has the potential for misuse and abuse depending on the practitioner.

American 20th century composer John Cage composed a piece of music in 1951 called *Music of Changes*, a reference to the Chinese method of divination, the I Ching, also known as the "Book of Changes". All of the compositional procedures in this piece were based on the idea of **chance operations**, a secular and skeptical code word for **divination**. In his piece "Music for Piano", Cage used paper imperfections to derive musical pitches and the I Ching to determine things like rhythm, dynamics, and various other elements of the arrangement. Later in his career he applied similar methods of musical divination to astrology charts, in his *Atlas Aclipticalis (1961-62), Etudes Australes (1974-75), Freeman Etudes (1977-90)*, and *Etudes Boreales (1978)*.

Cage would pose questions to the I Ching about the music composition procedures themselves. For example, he might ask for guidance about which modes to use, which of the twelve keys to compose in, and which notes of the given musical mode he ought to play at a given moment in the song. Like the translation of sacred names into musical notes, Cage translated the sacred symbolism of the I Ching (which resembles tarot imagery in its mythic and mystical qualities) into musical notes. The Tone Color Alchemy divination methods are based on similar principles.

Step 1. Posing a Question to the Oracle

The first stage of any divination process is to identify a focal point. The Tone Color Alchemy attributions are like symbol-mirrors reflecting back various aspects of the topic of inquiry. The revelations that come through divination may confirm something that we already suspected. They may also disclose thought-forms in our psyche that we had not yet realized were there or had not given due consideration. The more specific our question, the more likely we are to receive a strong intuitive response through meditation with the cards.

Step 2. Choosing a Divination Medium

Any variety of methods can be applied to the process of divination. The first involves work with the TCA cards as though they were tarot cards, laying them out in spreads, where each position in the spread has a pre-determined meaning. The cards then double as a method of acquiring knowledge and producing a seed-melody, so that the meaning of the musical seed-sigil derives its divinity not from a sacred name or entity, but from the oracular response of the operator's psyche, as expressed through the outwardly manifest medium of the cards. Alternatively, a person can divine through analysis of natal and transit charts, translating important aspects of a person's chart into musical harmonies. In this method, personal insights are still derived through traditional divinatory means, but the information is written in the stars rather than the spontaneous emergence of a tarot spread.

Step 3. Draw Your Own Conclusions

As you go through the process, notice the thoughts and feelings that come up in response to the symbols at hand. If they seem too vague, then continue to refine your questions until you have achieved the level of clarity that you were seeking. Ultimately, the answers are already there within you. Divination is a merely a technique of methodically invoking the omnipresent self-knowledge of your inner guidance.

Step 4. Make it Musical

Once you have a clear sense of the meaning of your cards, you can translate the symbols into musical notes and derive a musical seed sigil. If you get stuck along the way, you can always return to the cards and request guidance about how to continue in the piece. In this way, like John Cage, you can use divination to ask pragmatic questions about the music itself.

CARTOMANCY: TAROT DIVINATION

Much like songwriting, divination is a creative act. The process begins with a few simple signals or symbols that gradually develop into a more specific and information-rich transmission over the course of the reading. You may choose to address the Tone Color Alchemy cards with questions about your own life or the life of another. The overarching purpose of this work is to gain insight into a situation, and in the case of this particular method, to come out of the reading with a seed-sigil from which you could compose a piece of music, if you wish to do so.

How to Begin: It can be helpful to take a seat and get comfortable. With an upright spine and relaxed posture, begin with some deep breathing to calm the mind and sharpen your focus. Formulate your question clearly, either speaking it out loud or to yourself, within your mind, imagining that a trans-human, oracular intelligence is listening to you and has the intention to mirror back the perfect response to your inquiry. As you shuffle the cards, imagine that the oracle is omniscient and aware not only of which symbols you need to see, but where they are located in the deck, so that it will guide you through your intuitive feeling of when to stop shuffling. If you are reading for someone else, let them cut the deck so that their energy is infused into the session.

Past, Present, and Future: The subject matter of divination, especially when geared toward questions about personal matters such as love life and finances, will tend to be wrapped up in drama and strong emotions. These energies are usually some confluence of ruminations about the past, thoughts and feelings in the present, and projections into what may happen in the future. When conducting a reading, it can be helpful to stay in the present as much as possible, allowing the past and future to provide supplemental information without becoming the focal points of the working. Keep in mind that reading for another person comes with a lot of responsibility. Cartomancy is intended to be helpful and clarifying, so be sure to hold healing intentions for whomever you are working with, including yourself.

Tarot Spreads: Once you have posed your question to the oracle, shuffled the cards, and feel ready to move forward, the next step is to decide what kind of geometric layout, or "spread", would best suit your reading. Broad and general questions are typically paired with large spreads, while more specific questions tend to have more succinct answers and therefore can be accomplished with smaller spreads. Reading spreads may seem challenging at first, but if you move sequentially, step by step, and proceed creatively from the beginning to end, you are almost certain to derive significant information. Just keep in mind that the cards are trying to communicate a story to you through their own symbolic language. When first experimenting with cartomancy, it can be best to ask specific questions and work with simple spreads to avoid feeling overwhelmed by too many cards at once.

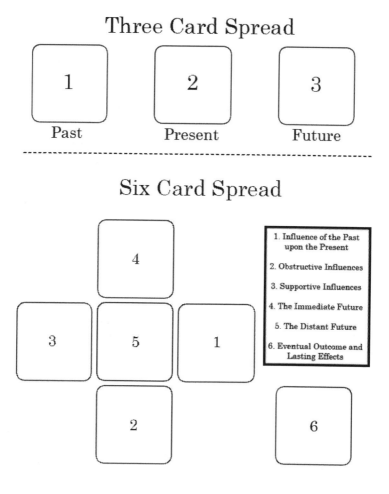

Three Card Spread

Six Card Spread

The Three Card Spread features a basic "Past-Present-Future" layout. Whatever card lands in these designated positions should be interpreted as the dominant energetic influence upon that area of the querent's life. The cross-shaped Six Card Spread elaborates upon these attributions, where the "distant future" takes center stage.

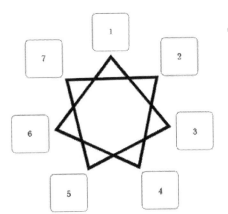

Seven Card Spread
The Weekly Forecast

1. Monday
2. Tuesday
3. Wednesday
4. Thursday
5. Friday
6. Saturday
7. Sunday

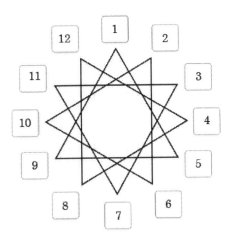

Twelve Card Spread
12 Month Forecast

1. January
2. February
3. March
4. April
5. May
6. June
7. July
8. August
9. September
10. October
11. November
12. December

For questions regarding short-term situations, the seven-day forecast can be a useful guide through your imagination and projections. Each day of the week is assigned one card that will determine the dominant energetic influence upon that day. Long-term situations and a general forecast for the year can be laid out as a Twelve Card Spread. In a similar way, each card in the spread represents one month of the year. You can also substitute the months with the astrological houses, so that January represents the qualities of the first house (querent's personality), February represents the second house (money and material possessions), and so forth through all twelve positions. For details about the meaning of each house, refer to the previous chapter on Astrology and the Planets, Signs and Houses.

Translating the Cards into Musical Notes

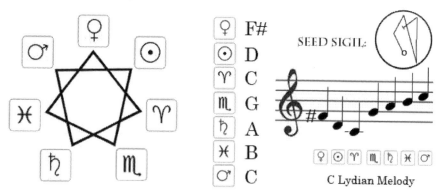

C Lydian Melody

In this particular example, I cast a seven card "weekly forecast" spread and translated them into musical notes through the standard Tone Color Alchemy method. The seven cards are a combination of planetary and zodiacal signs, each representing the dominant energy of the attributed day. When played in a linear sequence, moving clockwise around the seven points of the heptagram, the seven planets form a seven-note sequence.

Notice that Aries and Mars occupy the third and seventh positions respectively. Both are attributed to the tone color "C-Red" and therefore, when we translate them onto staff paper the musical note C appears twice in the seed melody. One could interpret this melodic sequence in a number of ways. It makes sense to pin it to the "Lydian" mode with a root note of C. The F# functions as an augmented fourth, a trademark of the Lydian mode, and the repetition of the note C, especially in the four-note stepwise ascent to C in the higher octave, reinforces the C note as a tonal center.

Overall, the purpose of consulting the Tone Color Alchemy cards as an oracle prior to extracting the seed melody is to infuse the melody with a deeper level of personal meaning and significance. Thoughts and feelings are critical food for the creative impulse, and while it would not be impossible to compose songs from randomly generated notes, there is something stimulating and exciting about knowing that the melody you choose to work with is intimately connected to your own life or the life of the person for whom you are divining.

ASTROLOGICAL DIVINATION

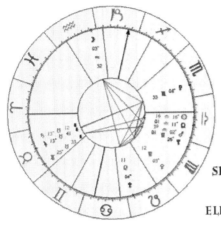

| HOUSE | SIGN | PLANET |

FIRST HOUSE : ♉ : ♅ ♃ ♄

FIFTH HOUSE : ♌ : ♀

SIXTH HOUSE : ♍ : ♆ ♀

♎ : ☉ ♂

SEVENTH HOUSE : ♏ : ☿

ELEVENTH HOUSE : ♒ : ☾

John Lennon's Natal Chart : October 9, 1940 @ 6:30 pm, Liverpool England

---

First House: Aries (C)
Fifth House: Leo (E)
Sixth House: Virgo (F)
Seventh House: Libra (F#)
Eighth House: Scorpio (G)
Eleventh House: Aquarius (A#)

Linear Sequence of the Houses

♉ : ♅ ♃ ♄ (C# : E, A#, A)

♌ : ♀ (E : C)

♍ : ♆ ♀ (F : G#, F#)

♎ : ☉ ♂ (F# : D, C)

♏ : ☿ (G : E)

♒ : ☾ (A# : G#)

(♅ ♃ ♄ ♀ ♆ ♀ ☉ ♂ ☿ ☾)

Linear Sequence of Planets + Signs

Translating Natal and Transit Charts into Music

I have already written in detail about the general mechanics of Astrology, including the tone color attributions to each planet and sign. The purpose of this section is to show more explicitly how a person's natal or transit chart can be converted into music, with John Lennon as our subject.

HOUSES: The musical notes associated with the houses are identical to the corresponding signs, so that 1st house corresponds to Aries (C-Red), 5th house to the fifth zodiacal sign, Leo (E-Yellow), 6th house to the sixth zodiacal sign, Virgo (F-Yellow-Green) and so forth. Moving counterclockwise along the circumference of the twelve houses, only those that are occupied by planets will be taken into consideration for the creation of a melody.

PLANETS AND SIGNS: The musical notes associated with the planets and signs have already been given in the previous chapter on astrology. When working with an astrological chart, you can either play the planetary melody by itself, arranging them in the same linear order as they appear during the counter-clockwise progression through houses, from first through twelfth, or you can play them in conjunction with the signs under which they appear. The visual demonstration above features the planets and signs notated in treble clef on the same staff.

ANALYSIS: A great deal of information could be said about John Lennon's personality based on what's available to us in his chart. His Pluto in Leo, for example, relates to his notorious case of stage fright. Despite performing live on stage thousands of times, he was still known to consistently throw up before a show. Each planet-sign pairing has its own unique meaning and could be cross-correlated with the details of his life to highlight aspects of his character.

Musically, the translation of John Lennon's chart into music evokes the following notes: C, C#, D, E, F, F#, G, G#, A, A#. The only two notes missing are D# and B. corresponding to Cancer and Pisces (the cardinal and mutable water signs). The emotional intensity of his song lyrics could be represented by the presence of Mercury in Scorpio, the fixed water sign. Musically, Mercury and Scorpio correlate to a minor third or major six interval between E and G. A composer could represent this aspect of his personality by composing a piece of music about him and emphasizing these two notes, either melodically or harmonically. This same basic principle could be applied to any of the notes attributed to the signs and planets.

Further details about the process of interpreting and translating natal charts are available through private Tone Color Alchemy consultations.

We are nearing the end of the road for this introductory text on Tone Color Alchemy. The majority of the work so far has dealt with attributing a vast network of symbolic correspondences to the standard 12-tone palette of Western music. Information of all kinds can be translated into musical notes so that the subsequent melodies are imbued with a mythic and psycho-active subtext that informs the mood of the creative process while also providing a kind of "hidden meaning" that only the initiated would recognize and appreciate. In keeping with the Kabbalistic tradition, everything connects to everything and everything mirrors everything, so that with enough contemplation, all melodies are revealed to be part of a unified field of meta-physical interconnectivity.

Unification of opposites is the main goal of all great Western alchemical operations, as evidenced in the central axiom *"Solve et Coagula"* or "dissolve and coagulate". To separate something into its parts and then bring it back together is to eat from the tree of knowledge and discover the building blocks of life. According to the lineage, lead is transmuted into gold through this very process. With the aid of the elements, appropriate lab equipment, and the philosopher's stone, transmutation of actual physical substances becomes possible. The Tone Color Alchemy method aims to reveal how musicians naturally engage this same process, regardless of whether they literally experiment with magical correspondence tables. Our imagination, being the source of all great musical expression, amounts to a kind of inspirited symbolic dialogue between the Self and the self. Our role as artist/shaman is to get out of the way and allow the influence of a transcendent force to possess us long enough to channel the upper-dimensional visionary realms into 4-D consensus reality.

Both the kabbalists and great musician-composers of the West seek satisfaction through playful delineation and recombination of their preferred symbolic building blocks (alphabet and musical notes). Ideally, they will eventually achieve a level of completion in the Great Work that brings their mind and heart to a state of rest. This is where the cultivation of compassion comes in to the picture. The innermost teachings of Judaism are about compassion and ethical behavior. Like a positive feedback loop that feeds upon good intention and reciprocates with miracles and blessings, unconditional love for others is key to receiving support from the universe to continue our work.

CULTIVATING COMPASSION

Tibetan Buddhist Mantras

Although innumerable incantations and words of power exist in the Western hermetic tradition, I have always held an eclectic attitude toward spiritual practice. So when it comes to chanting mantra, something deep within me felt pulled beyond the confines of Greek and Jewish mysticism. A few years ago I was introduced by one of my mentors to a lineage of Tibetan Buddhism that radically altered the way I worked with prayer and mantra. Vocalizing sacred words in a ceremonial context has a transformative effect upon the way I feel and the kind of thoughts that pass through my mind. Before and after my songwriting process, I like to sit at an **altar** and pray. It's one of the best ways I've found to enter an **"altered" state** without the use of psychoactive drugs. In contrast to the highly mental process translation between words and musical notes, mantra is a time in my life where I let go of the twelve-tone system and surrender to the act of singing. One of my favorite mind-melting mantras is the Heart Sutra:

"O Shariputra! Form is emptiness and emptiness is form. Form is none other than emptiness and emptiness none other than form. The same is true for feelings, conceptions, impulses and consciousness. O Shariputra, the characteristics of the void are not created, not annihilated, not impure, not pure, not increasing, not decreasing. Therefore, in the void there are no forms and no feelings, no conceptions, no impulses and no consciousness. There is no eye, no ear, no nose, tongue, no body or mind; There is no form, no sound, no smell, no taste, no touch, no ideas; no eye element, no min element, and no mind consciousness element; no ignorance and no end of ignorance, no old age and death; no end of old age and death. Likewise, there is no suffering, no cause of suffering, and no cessation of suffering. There is no wisdom and no attainment whatsoever.

"Because there is nothing to be attained, a boddhisatva relying on Prajnaparamita has no obstruction in his heart. Because there is no obstruction, he has no fear and passes beyond all confused imagination, reaching the Ultimate Nirvana. All buddhas in the past, present and future have attained Supreme Enlightenment by relying on Prajnaparamita. Therefore we know that the Prajnaparamita is the great magic Mantra, the great Mantra of Illumination, it is the supreme mantra, the unequaled mantra which can truly extinguish all suffering without fail. Therefore, he uttered the prajnaparamita mantra, saying:

"Tadyatha Om Gate Gate Paragate Parasamgate Boddhi Svaha"

Dedication of the Merit

I would like to share one final transmission, a Tibetan mantra called the Dedication of the Merit, which offers up whatever merit and blessings have been accumulated during one's practice for the benefit of all beings. In a similar way, I wish to offer whatever merit I have accumulated through independent study and the writing of this book, so that others may receive benefit from it in whatever way they see fit.

Sonam Diyi Tamche Zigpa Nyi

Tobne nyepe dranam pam che te

Kye ga na shi balab trugpa yi

Sipe tsole drow dolwar sho

- - -

By this merit may all beings obtain omniscience

May it defeat the enemy of wrongdoing

From the turbulent waves of

Birth, old age, sickness, death, the ocean of Samsara

May all beings be set free!

FEATURING WRITERS FROM: THE SYNC WHOLE, REALITY SANDWICH

ETEMENANKI, THE MASK OF GOD, LABYRINTH OF THE PSYCHONAUT, KOZMIKON, LIVE FROM THE LOGOSPHERE, STAR THEORY

A FEW SHOTS TO SHAMAN, LIBYAN SIBYL, ACCIDENTAL ALCHEMIST, THE STYGIAN PORT, CONSTELLATION CONTEMPLATION.

THE SYNC BOOK

FEATURING 26 AUTHORS ON SYNCHRONICITY

EDITED BY ALAN ABBADESSA GREEN

MYTHS, MAGIC, MEDIA, AND MINDSCAPES

WRITTEN BY:

ALAN ABBADESSA-GREEN + GORO ADACHI + JASON BARRERA

DOUGLAS BOLLES + PEG CARTER + TOMMY FULKS + KEVIN HALCOTT

KYLE HUNT + SIBYL HUNTER + STEFAN JABLONSKI + JEREMY

ANDRAS JONES + CRYSTAL KANARR + JON KIDD + JAKE KOTZE

NEIL KRAMER + RAMMER MARTÍNEZ + JUSTIN MORGAN + WILL MORGAN

CHRISTOPHER MYERS + EUNUS NOE + JENNIFER PALMER

JIM SANDERS + MICHAEL SCHACHT + TOURE + STEVE WILLNER

THE PATTERNIST, GOSPORN, ALL THE HAPPY CREATURES, KOSMOS IDIKOS

TWENTY-SIX AUTHORS ON SYNCHRONICITY

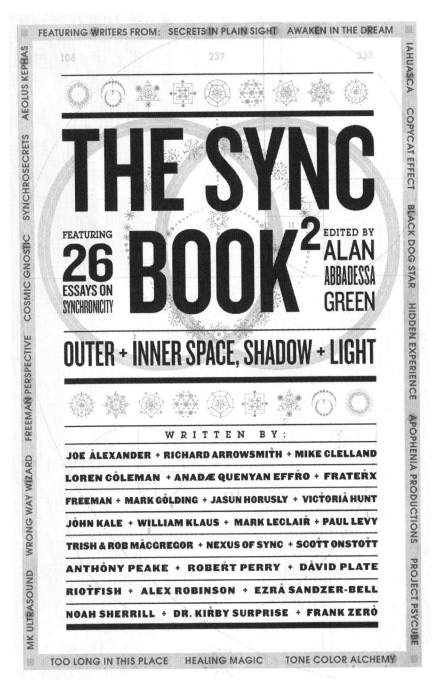

FEATURING WRITERS FROM: SECRETS IN PLAIN SIGHT   AWAKEN IN THE DREAM

108   237   333

IAHUASCA

COPYCAT EFFECT

BLACK DOG STAR

HIDDEN EXPERIENCE

APOPHENIA PRODUCTIONS

PROJECT PSYCUBE

AEOLUS KEPHAS

SYNCHROSECRETS

COSMIC GNOSTIC

FREEMAN PERSPECTIVE

WRONG WAY WIZARD

MK ULTRASOUND

THE SYNC BOOK²

FEATURING
26
ESSAYS ON
SYNCHRONICITY

EDITED BY
ALAN ABBADESSA GREEN

OUTER + INNER SPACE, SHADOW + LIGHT

WRITTEN BY:

JOE ALEXANDER + RICHARD ARROWSMITH + MIKE CLELLAND

LOREN COLEMAN + ANADÆ QUENYAN EFFRO + FRATERX

FREEMAN + MARK GOLDING + JASUN HORUSLY + VICTORIA HUNT

JOHN KALE + WILLIAM KLAUS + MARK LECLAIR + PAUL LEVY

TRISH & ROB MACGREGOR + NEXUS OF SYNC + SCOTT ONSTOTT

ANTHONY PEAKE + ROBERT PERRY + DAVID PLATE

RIOTFISH + ALEX ROBINSON + EZRA SANDZER-BELL

NOAH SHERRILL + DR. KIRBY SURPRISE + FRANK ZERO

TOO LONG IN THIS PLACE   HEALING MAGIC   TONE COLOR ALCHEMY

ALL NEW AUTHORS:
TWENTY-SIX ESSAYS ON SYNCHRONICITY

ACCIDENTAL

ANDRAS

JONES

INITIATIONS

In The Kabbalistic Tree of Olympia

Winter's Labyrinth

a novella in four parts

Douglas Bolles

A CIRCUITOUS ADVENTURE OF SELF DISCOVERY

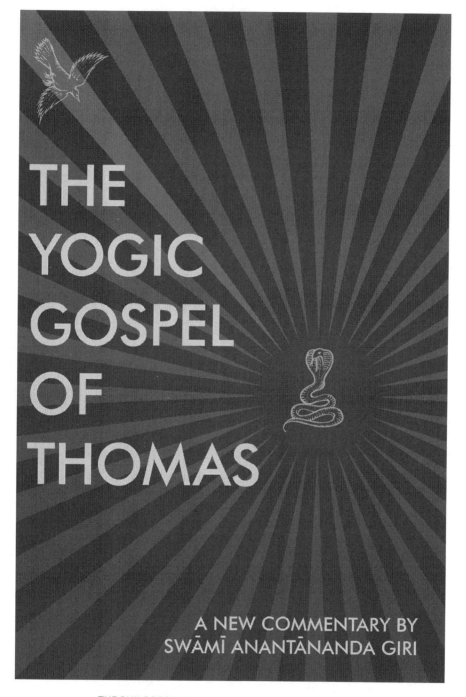

THE YOGIC GOSPEL OF THOMAS

A NEW COMMENTARY BY
SWĀMĪ ANANTĀNANDA GIRI

THE PHILOSOPHICAL COMMON GROUND BETWEEN
THE GOSPEL OF THOMAS AND THE YOGIC MYSTICISM OF INDIA

THE
SECRET
WAR INSIDE
FREEMASONRY

FRATER X

IN A WAR FOR CONTROL, A WAR FOR YOUR MIND,
A SECRET SOCIETY HIDES NOTHING MORE THAN ITS INNER STRUGGLE

SUICIDE KINGS

ATOR ROTA ORAT TORA TARO

ALAN ABBADESSA-GREEN

HOW SYNCHRONICITY AND ARCHETYPES EMERGE IN WORLD EVENTS:
FROM THE JFK ASSASSINATION TO 9/11 AND THE DEATH OF OSAMA BIN LADEN

SYNC BOOK PRESS

SYNCBOOKPRESS.COM

25231062R00124

Made in the USA
Middletown, DE
22 October 2015